GALA PERFORMANCE

Gala Performance

EDITED BY

Arnold Haskell

Mark Bonham Carter

Michael Wood

With a Foreword by
H.R.H. The Princess Margaret

COLLINS
ST JAMES'S PLACE, LONDON
1955

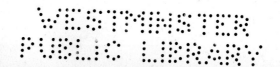

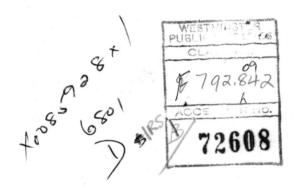
PRINTED IN GREAT BRITAIN
TEXT AND COLOUR PRINTED AND THE BOOK BOUND BY
WILLIAM COLLINS SONS AND CO. LTD., LONDON AND GLASGOW
MONOCHROME PHOTOGRAVURE SECTIONS PRINTED BY
HARRISON AND SONS LTD., HIGH WYCOMBE, BUCKS.

Acknowledgments

THE EDITORS of *Gala Performance* are deeply grateful to all who have contributed so generously with their time and skill. They have benefited the dancers of the future for whose assistance this volume was conceived.

The Editors are especially grateful to H.R.H. The Princess Margaret for her message of good wishes and for permission to reproduce her photograph as a frontispiece.

In particular, they wish to thank Dame Ninette de Valois, Mr. William Chappell, Sir Kenneth Clark, Mr. Robert Irving, Mr. James Monahan, and Mr. Sacheverell Sitwell who have contributed articles to *Gala Performance*; and Mr. Edward Burra, M. Antoni Clavé, Mr. John Craxton, Mr. Robin Ironside, Mr. Osbert Lancaster, Mr. Oliver Messel, and Mr. John Piper who have allowed their designs to be reproduced in colour; and also W. H. Alden, Derek Allen, Gordon Anthony, Jitendra Arya, John Baker, Baron, Cecil Beaton, J. W. Debenham, Denis de Marney, Felix Fonteyn, Harrods Ltd., John Hart, Herbert Lambert, Angus McBean, Edward Mandinian, Mesdames Morter, Melton Pippin, Richardby, Houston Rogers, Maurice Seymour, Dudley Styles, Paul Tanqueray, Tunbridge-Sedgwick, Vaughan & Freeman, Vivienne, G. B. L. Wilson, and Roger Wood who have contributed photographs. These contributors have generously foregone any payment in favour of the Sadler's Wells Benevolent Fund.

The Editors owe much to those who have assisted in the research required for this book including Miss Mary Clarke, Miss Burchell (Honorary Librarian, Vic-Wells Association), The Honourable Eveleigh Leith, Miss Joan Lawson, and Mr. Cyril Beaumont.

Thanks are due to Mlle. Lucienne Astruc, Mrs. Wilfred de Glehn, Mr. James de Rothschild, M. Serge Lifar, Mr. W. B. Morris, Mme. Bertha Nicolas, Mr. Laurence Whistler, and Mr. Peter Williams who have given permission for property in their possession to be photographed and reproduced in this book; and to A. & C. Black Ltd., the British Council, *Daily Graphic*, *Evening Standard*, International News Photos, Odhams Press Ltd., and the Photo Repro Company who have kindly allowed photographs in their possession to be used.

Contents

FOREWORD   *page* 11
by H.R.H. The Princess Margaret

PROLOGUE   13
by Sacheverell Sitwell

EARLY DAYS, AN ALBUM WITH NOTES   37
by William Chappell

THE SADLER'S WELLS SCHOOL   55
by Arnold Haskell

THE SCHOOL   67
Photographs

THE SADLER'S WELLS BALLET   75
by James Monahan

THE SADLER'S WELLS THEATRE BALLET   75
Photographs

THE SADLER'S WELLS BALLET, COVENT GARDEN   91
Photographs

MUSIC AND THE BALLET   117
by Robert Irving

MUSIC   125
Photographs

BALLET DECORS   133
by Sir Kenneth Clark

SETS AND COSTUMES   139
Photographs

SOME PROBLEMS OF BALLET TODAY   page 158
    by Dame Ninette de Valois

MASKS AND FACES   161
    Photographs

APPENDIX   201
    Details of Ballets performed 1939-1955

INDEX   243

Colour Plates

H.R.H. The Princess Margaret
Photograph by Cecil Beaton   *frontispiece*

Design for *Job* by John Piper   *facing page* 32

Front cloth for *Don Quixote* by Edward Burra   65

Front cloth for *Ballabile* by Antoni Clavé   80

Sketches for *Daphnis and Chloé* by John Craxton   97

Robin Ironside's design for *Sylvia*   112

Osbert Lancaster's design for Act I of *Coppelia*   145

Costume designs for *Homage to the Queen* by Oliver Messel   160

Foreword

BY H.R.H. THE PRINCESS MARGARET

As PRESIDENT of the Sadler's Wells Foundation I am delighted to write the Foreword to *Gala Performance*. The success of British ballet is something of which we all have reason to be proud. It has attained the status of a national institution after a very brief career, and it has grown from very small beginnings.

Gala Performance is a tribute to all those who have shared in this achievement, whether or not they are mentioned in its pages. The writers, artists and photographers whose work appears in this book have made their contributions without payment, and the royalties from the book will go towards an endowment for the Sadler's Wells School. All of us who love the ballet, and who are proud of the great reputation won by the Sadler's Wells in Britain and all over the world, will be happy to help the dancers of the future by buying this book.

May, 1955

Margaret

PROLOGUE

Sacheverell Sitwell

IN the lives of all persons of sensibility there are certain territories of the spirit which are our public and private possessions, to be as hotly defended as our own homes. This is not the same feeling as an interest in some particular game or sport. It is more lasting and more sacred. A love for the theatre can be one of the strongest of all these mental and spiritual attachments. There is love for the theatre pure and simple, which is the play; and the audience for Orpheus and his Lyre, by which opera is intended. There are the followers, too, and daily they grow more numerous, of Terpsichore. My classical dictionary describes her as "one of the Muses, daughter of Jupiter. She presided over dancing, of which she was reckoned the inventress, as her name intimates, and with which she delighted her sisters. She is represented like a young virgin crowned with laurel, and holding in her hand a musical instrument." Her London address is, at present, 54, Colet Gardens, home of the Sadler's Wells School; and the worthy object of this present volume is to extend her premises and provide lodging and instruction for her devotees. Ballet has now settled permanently in London. Pupils come to the school from every part of Great Britain and from Overseas; and perhaps the purposes of this book need no further explanation than photographs of the children of the school at work and play. The Sadler's Wells School has, already, fine and commodious premises, but these must be enlarged in order to provide a home for more.

Having stated the theme, we now begin the variations. For this is to be a personal account of what the spectacle of dancing has meant in the life and enjoyment of one particular writer and member of the audience, and as such it has to be to some little extent autobiographical, which the reader must excuse because of the special exigencies of the case, the specialized nature of these pages, and the call upon all of us who know or remember a little to write down our memories before it is too late. What can become a lifelong passion can be brought to one's attention in a haphazard way. I have often thought that a special predilection in my own life for the 18th century, which I am too lazy to deny, arose from the circumstances of my being woken up in the middle of the night when I was about eight or nine years old, in a bedroom in the Hotel Minerva in Florence, by the magical chiming of a minuet or gavotte. I listened spellbound, unable to move or stir, not knowing where it came from. Would it play again? No, no. And I imagined it was for that once, and gone for ever. But later it played again, and with it a little chiming bell that struck two or three little strokes when the tune had ended. I have that minuet or gavotte in my ear, now, as I write this, although it was so long ago. What had happened was that my father, returning from Lucca where he had been making a round of the curiosity shops, had bought this clock among other things, and his valet Henry Moat, having no other place to put it, had stored it in a drawer in my bedroom. I remember the clock for a long time after that in our house in Scarborough, though I cannot have heard it since 1922, and do not know, now, what has happened to it.

So do little things come into one's life and make a difference to that. Or they can 'enter' in the grand way as though sure of themselves and of their effect upon the victim. I have written before, in another place, of the grand events so important in my childhood which occurred on Christmas Day in 1905. My family had rented a villa at San Remo because my brother had been ill with pleurisy; and on that Christmas Day we drove over to Monte Carlo in a motor, the first time I had driven in one; we were taken to a theatre, the 'golden' theatre of Garnier in the Casino, the first time I had ever been inside a theatre, but this was for a concert; and we heard *Casse-Noisette*. That same experience of hearing Tchaikowsky's music for *Casse-Noisette* for the first time, must, I think, have been a magical sensation for many other persons. It opens a whole new world to one; the world of the dance and the theatre. It is the *Danse des Mirlitons* and the *Valse des Fleurs* that one remembers most from *Casse-Noisette*. And at about the same time the waltz from Tchaikowsky's *La Belle au Bois dormant* first came to my ears. I heard it on the pianola in my grandmother's house in Surrey. I consider these early sensations of Tchaikowsky's music to have been my first introduction to the magical world of Russian Ballet. One knew this was ballet music though one did not know the names of any Russian dancers. Nor was it the mere question of not being old enough to know about such matters for even Pavlova had not yet appeared in England. It is, in fact, a source of much pride to myself that Anna Pavlova had made her first appearance in England on a stage specially constructed in the ballroom at St. Dunstans, Regent's Park, a house which at that time belonged to Lord Londesborough, who was my mother's brother. She had been performing at the Châtelet Theatre in Paris, under Diaghilev, and my uncle engaged her to dance after dinner before King Edward VII and Queen Alexandra. My uncle had previously seen her dance in Russia which he had recently visited. One is proud of any personal link, however tenuous, with the great days of the Ballets Russes. A year later, in April 1910, Pavlova and Mordkin made their début at the Palace Theatre and in one night became the rage of London.

In the following year, 1911, Serge de Diaghilev brought his company to London for the first time. They gave two seasons at Covent Garden, and from that year they appeared every year until the War. My own opportunities of seeing them while I was a schoolboy were very limited. The only chance was during Long Leave from Eton, when I was taken by my brother, then an ensign in the Grenadier Guards and stationed at Wellington Barracks or the Tower of London. He was twenty years old, and I was fifteen. In this way I saw *Le Spectre de la Rose* with Nijinski and Karsavina, and *l'Oiseau de Feu* in the same evening;* and in the next year (1913) heard Chaliapin in *Khovantchina*, at Drury Lane. This, too, was an astonishing experience, and I will never forget the extraordinary effect of Moussorgsky's brass instruments, and of the Russian choruses. Of course by that time I was already convinced that an art movement was coming out of Russia. One was converted in a night by their great artists. The next year, which was the year the War began, there was for some reason no ballet on the Friday, and only *La Bohème* on the Saturday night, so these were my only chances of seeing the now mythical Russian Opera and Russian Ballet in the pre-war years.

But of course I was told all about them by my brother. I well remember his descriptions of *Boris Godounov* and of *Prince Igor*, and I had begun collecting souvenir programmes. My sister, I remember, particularly admired Goncharova's setting for *Le Coq d'Or*, and I cannot doubt that the backcloth with its brightly coloured town had some effect upon her early poems. Another epoch-making event was Bakst's Persian setting for *Schéhérazade*. You never knew what Bakst would do next; there was his Hindoo setting for *Le Dieu Bleu* (one of the very few Russian Ballets that I have not seen), and almost in the same moment his early Victorian dresses for Schumann's *Carnaval*, and his classical backgrounds for *Daphnis et Chloé* and for *Narcisse*. Indeed much of my time as a schoolboy was actually spent in just this venture of wondering what Bakst really *would* do next; and now after more than half a lifetime spent in thinking of such things the only hero of my youth still to assert this same power upon me is Picasso.

Petrouchka must have been in many ways the supreme Russian Ballet. No artist in any of the arts who saw it could have been unaffected by it. I was often told about it, but was not to know the music, surely Stravinsky's masterpiece, until later. I was told, also, about *l'Après-midi d'un Faune*, knowing much of Debussy's music already for my sister played it on the piano. I remember less about the sensation caused by *Le Sacre du Printemps;* but I can recall descriptions of Bakst's Venetian costumes for *La Légende de Joseph* (another ballet I have not seen) in the style of Paul Veronese, and of Sert's background with the twisted columns.

On a blazing hot summer day during one of these Long Leaves I was taken to see an exhibition of Bakst's drawings at the Fine Art Society's Galleries in New Bond Street, and soon afterwards my brother bought *The Decorative Art* of Léon Bakst for the, then, staggering sum of four guineas. That was in 1913, now forty years ago, and in the same year having previously corresponded with him and bought some of the books on Russian Ballet that he published, or rather brought over from Paris, I walked boldly into the bookshop at 75, Charing Cross Road and emerged having made a new but perennial friend of Mr. C. W. Beaumont, on whose premises, since then, I have passed so many hours of pleasant conversation on our mutual interests and enthusiasms that they must add up to a total of several

* It will have been during the short autumn season of 1913 that my brother sat next in the stalls to Mr. C. P. Little, a dear old man who was social correspondent of one of the weekly papers. *L'Oiseau de Feu* was in performance, and when Karsavina made her matchless entrance as the Firebird he turned to my brother and asked him what news he had of the grouse season. The music of *L'Oiseau de Feu*, which I found impossible to master at a first hearing, was probably, after that of *Boris Godounov* and *Khovantchina* the most violent sensation of the pre-war Russian seasons.

entire weeks, or even months, over these many years. My interests were, now, fairly launched and have never lapsed or failed.

I believe I already knew the Russian Ballet programmes by heart; and there were as well the books of drawings of Nijinski and of Karsavina by George Barbier, and the magnificent and very expensive numbers of *La Gazette du Bon Ton*, coming out every month for ten shillings a number, with hand-coloured fashion drawings by Barbier and Lepape done by the *pochoir* process. This paper had constant articles on the Ballets Russes, and there were even occasional fashion drawings by Léon Bakst. One of them, depicting a young woman in the fashion of 1913 with much gold and silver in her dress, and holding a telephone, which would, by now, be a 'collector's piece' in itself, seemed to me to be the last word in daring modernity. I have, still, an almost complete run of *La Gazette du Bon Ton*, including the few and less characteristic numbers when it was revived after the War had ended. But the War had begun, by now, and almost the only links with those past glories were the early gramophone records of Sir Thomas Beecham. The Overture and March from *Prince Igor* came out in 1915, I think. My brother, who was back on leave from France, was made quite ill by hearing them for they so much recalled the lost and gone world of peace. On occasion, too, the music of *Schéhérazade* would be given at the Albert Hall, and I can remember not being able to think of anything else for hours beforehand because of this treat in store. That was in 1915 or 1916, just before I, myself, left school at Eton and went into the army.

To young persons of my age, I was then nineteen years old, there was an absolutely immeasurable gulf separating 1914 from 1917. There seemed to be little or no reason why the War should ever end. In company with my brother and sister I had begun writing, and my first book of poems was published in June 1918. We were making friends with a number of painters, writers and musicians, and among a majority of these it is only fair to say that the Russian Ballet was looked down upon as being too 'fashionable'. But this did not in the least alter my own opinion of it, and I remember thinking it might only be because so few of the Bloomsbury set ever put foot inside a theatre. This was, in fact, true. Covent Garden and Drury Lane had too many associations with tiaras and white ties. Roger Fry, for instance, hardly liked to hear mention of the name of Bakst. The region of Covent Garden and Drury Lane was, even then, for myself, a sacred area, as it could be, the precincts of two temples. Nothing, it seems, can alter the 'piazza', as it should be called, of Covent Garden. Neither bombs, nor the forces of demolition, can prevent it remaining much as it was in the time of Hogarth, an area haunted by the ghosts of Peg Woffington, of Edmund Kean, and many other shades. In 1917 Sir Thomas Beecham gave a season of opera at Covent Garden, including a beautiful production of *Nozze di Figaro* by Hugo Rumbold. I seem to have gone ten, or even twenty times to hear Figaro; and remember one particular performance when bombs were falling and above the music you could hear the anti-aircraft cannonade, though only a foretaste of worse things to come in that incredible fulfilment of two world wars within the span of one single generation.

Half of my school friends had been killed by now, and the War had become a fearful bloodbath.

It is necessary to say that one did not hear much of Diaghilev in those days. I was, by now, in the training battalion at Albuhera Barracks, Aldershot. Most of the recruits were young boys of eighteen or nineteen, many of them miners from South Yorkshire and Derbyshire, in fact, from near my old home, and I can still hear their North Country voices. There was a farewell parade when several hundreds of them entrained for Southampton to go to France, and I well remember the band playing *The British Grenadiers*, and the Commanding Officer saying afterwards in a broken voice that few of them would be living in a few weeks' time. Unfortunately, this was but too true. I am now thinking of August 1918. The awfulness of those concluding months of the War, and the apparent hopelessness of the outlook, had the effect of driving one in upon oneself and making one hold, more than ever, to what one

Costume design for the Chief Eunuch in 'Schéhérazade' by Léon Bakst

loved and valued. Somehow or other I contrived to write poetry at Aldershot, but my mental and spiritual recreation was in the news that Diaghilev and his company were about to return to London. This incredible information circulated early in the summer of 1918. Mr. Beaumont, in one of his books, states that the advertisement of their impending return appeared in the daily press of Monday, 29 July, but I was certainly told of it in May or June. All one knew was that they had spent much of the War in Spain where only two theatres, in Madrid and in Barcelona, were big enough for them to dance in, and that their being able to continue at all was due to the kindness of King Alfonso. They were announced as due to appear 'next week', but it was postponed, week by week, and so time dragged through the month of August.

It was an augury of Peace, and at the time there seemed to be no other. Even earlier that summer, however, while walking along Chelsea Embankment with my brother, on a Sunday morning during a respite from Chelsea Barracks, we passed an 'artist' with long hair, a bow tie, and pointed shoes, and my brother announced to me that this was the first good sign he had seen and that we would have Peace before many months were over. It was Stuart Hill, afterwards to become known as a portrait painter and he was, authentically, in this instance, the dove of Peace. Meanwhile, at Aldershot, where I was sent a little later, I became ever more futile in military life, and would spend hours on the Plain thinking of Gabriele d'Annunzio, whom I, then, esteemed as the greatest living writer, and wondering in a fever of expectation about the return of Diaghilev to London. My military incapacity must have been infuriating, but so few of my brother's contemporaries who were pre-war officers were still alive, that my superiors treated me with kindness. On one occasion, on a manœuvre, the Commanding Officer told me to take his bicycle and ride off with it to deliver a message. I had never been taught to ride a bicycle, nor had I even handled one, so that I had to walk away wheeling this unfamiliar object, but even that piece of futility and ignorance brought down no wrath upon me. *Le Coq d'Or* had been given by Sir Thomas Beecham a few weeks before this at Covent Garden, and Aldershot Plain is still associated in my mind with King Dodon, with the march and astrologer's song, and with the crowing of the golden cockerel. Also, and necessarily, with the Russian Revolution. I was young enough to think this made a great art movement

Tamara Karsavina as Columbine in 'Carnaval' by de Glehn

coming out of Russia more certain than ever; but my brother, a few years older than myself, was more far seeing and saw in it an un-mitigated disaster to the arts in Russia.

August was endless. Almost every day there were postponements. And then I remember one day being told that Diaghilev had arrived in London. The first night of the Coliseum was 5 September, and it was the *première* of *The Good Humoured Ladies*. The scenery was by Bakst, even then reputed to be out of favour with Diaghilev, and with my own childhood memories of Venice to compare to it I found this disappointing. But the dancing of Lydia Lopokova, of Idzikowsky, and of Miassine was a revelation. It was the first of Miassine's ballets to be performed in London; and his name was still spelt with two 'i's,

Miassine, and not yet Massine. It was the speed of the dancing that was irresistible, especially in the famous supper scene. Bakst was reported to have been ill for months, on and off, with nervous breakdown, and his dresses and scenery in my opinion bore signs of this. His scene was not at all Venetian; Lopokova's dress as *Mariuccia* was charming; but the huge wig and false nose of Josephine Cecchetti as *Marquise Silvestra* were irritating and exaggerated. I felt that the great day of my hero Bakst was over. I do not think Bakst came to London during this first season, or I would have met him. That great musician Mrs. Gordon Woodhouse, who was already a friend of ours, often played the famous Domenico Scarlatti Sonata No. 345 in A major, Longo Edition, with the crossed hands, and I found the rapidity of thought in Scarlatti and the sparkling tones of the harpsichord ill matched with Bakst's conception. Lydia Lopokova we met at Violet Woodhouse's in Ovington Square; and not long afterwards went to tea with her in her flat in Savoy Court where she had many little birds in cages. No person at all resembling Lydia Lopokova has appeared again during my experience of ballet, and it is perhaps impossible to reproduce her quick wit, her peculiar use of English, and personal fascination. I was, then, and for some more months, or years, too shy to talk.

During the matinée performances at the Coliseum *Cléopâtre* was given, with ugly scenery by Robert Delaunay. Massine appeared in this with Lubov Tchernicheva, and the music was a conglomerate of Rimsky-Korsakov and Glazounov. Some of the original pre-war costumes of the Bakst production were still used and the results were incongruous. For Cleopatra's dress was by Sonia Delaunay; and Diaghilev, who must have been dissatisfied with the presentation, later in the season added a backcloth by, I think, the London painter Alfred Wolmark, which was but little of an improvement. I came up as often as possible from Aldershot, probably even two or even three times a week, to see the performances, and went back by the last train, arriving at about 1.30 a.m. which was, then, a late hour for me, followed by a long walk from the station to barracks for there were never taxis.

One ballet only was given each evening, sandwiched in between music hall turns. Always arriving punctually when the performance began, for I could not bear to miss a moment of it, there was, I have to admit, a certain turn during which I always walked out and took refuge in the foyer. This was when the curtain rose, and a solemn faced young man stood in the middle of the stage with the spotlight upon him playing his violin. I was serious minded and this was too much for me. It was always some terribly trite and sentimental tune that he began playing, with strained intensity of expression, sometimes, I think, *Roses of Picardy*, and fearing worse things to come I would give up my seat. It was only after many weeks of this, that hearing howls and gales of laughter beginning only a moment or two after my departure I decided to stay behind, and sit it out, and see what happened. It was Grock and his partner whom I had missed so often in this fashion. Meanwhile, other ballets were added week by week to the repertoire. *Carnaval* was put on, and the Polovtsian dances from *Prince Igor*.

One of the major excitements, in thinking of which I spent days and weeks of expectation during a 'gas-course', was the revival of *Schéhérazade*. This took place on 11 October, a never to be forgotten evening, but, even so, it was a little disappointing. Although I had never seen it before, it was obvious that the production was poor compared with the original (1910) performance. I knew well the setting for that, from coloured illustration. The huge hanging lamps were gone, and also the marvellous green tone of Bakst's original scenery, which was one of the epoch making events in theatrical history, as important to the theatre, scenically, as *Le Sacre du Printemps* was important, musically. The production of *Carnaval* was more to my own personal satisfaction. Lydia Lopokova with her fair hair in ringlets made an appealing Columbine, and Harlequin was Idzikowski. Although I never saw Nijinski in this rôle my instinct tells me that Mr. Beaumont is right when he says that Idzikowski "was inclined to exaggerate the shaking of the head, and swing it in a wide arc, whereas Nijinski's head movement was so momentary and so exquisitely timed that it had all the force of a mark of exclamation." Nijinski's smiles, he says, "were fleeting and tinged with mockery." *Sadko*, with most of its action taking place at the bottom of the sea, was another production of this season; and it was preceded by *The Enchanted Princess*, or in fact, the famous 'Blue Bird' *pas de deux* from *La Belle au Bois Dormant*. This was danced by Lopokova and Idzikowski, and it belonged to another world, that of real dancing. Later productions were *The Midnight Sun* on 21 November, just after the blessed Armistice, and *Children's Tales* on 23 December. *Les Sylphides* was given, also, but I avoided it, for I hate Chopin orchestrated, and the performance too much resembled a sweetened glass of synthetic lemonade. Nor did I, in fact, much care for *Children's Tales*, with Idzikowski as the cat, and Lydia Sokolova as Kikimora. The drop curtain by Larionov with its conventionalized flowers was in Russian peasant style, while the three tall ogres with their beards of gardener's bast were reminiscent of our friend Lytton Strachey, whose portrait, now in the Tate Gallery, was being painted at about that time by Henry Lamb. *The Midnight Sun* which was, in fact, Massine's first ballet had colourful and fanciful dresses by Larionov. The corps-de-ballet wore *Kokoshniks* (tall headdresses) which were bright and glittering with tinsel. But the choreography was curious and Massine, himself, clashing a pair of paper cymbals together as he danced, seemed as though he had wandered from an Italian fairground to the shores of Lapland. The season continued with great success until the end of March 1919, and the repertoire was now fairly re-established.

But I must now write of Diaghilev, himself, instigator and promoter of so many wonders. Owing to a surfeit of excitement, for I know he was pointed out to me and I was introduced to him and shook his hand, I remember nothing of Diaghilev on the first night. However, I went so often to the Coliseum on the following weeks that in imagination I am still there, and can never go down St. Martin's Lane without remembering the innumerable performances of Russian Ballet I have seen in that theatre. I think the truth is that excepting for the dancing of Lopokova and Massine in *The Good Humoured Ladies* the

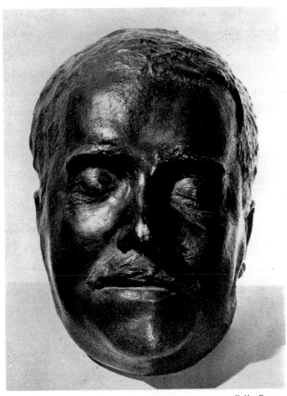

Death mask of Serge Diaghilev presented to the Bibliothèque de l'Opéra de Paris by Serge Lifar

company was a little weak during this first season at the Coliseum. We soon got to know Diaghilev well. He came several times, perhaps on five or six occasions in all, to the house my brother and I shared in Swan Walk, Chelsea. After the first revival of *Schéhérazade*, early in October, there was a supper party somewhere, and Diaghilev heard me making excuses for not being able to go, saying as was the sad truth, that I had to get back to Aldershot. He must have heard me say this before, for he immediately asked, "*Qu'est ce que c'est, cette 'Aldershot'? C'est le nom de votre maîtresse?*" For a long time, thinking that the abbreviated form of my christian name, which is 'Sachie', was 'Sasha', he called me, in Russian fashion, 'Alexander'. We met Diaghilev, also, in the houses of several mutual friends. He was at that time about forty-eight years old, but with his Russian pallor and white lock of hair looked ageless, and neither young, nor old. He was tallish, about five foot ten, and always immaculately dressed for evening performances, with white tie, white waistcoat with pearl stud, opera hat, and eyeglass. Two things that you noticed about him, physically, were his large head and his small hands. He was very proud of his resemblance to Peter the Great, and always delighted to be told that he resembled the great Tsar. He, in fact, claimed to be descended from him, and it is true that he resembled the famous bust of Peter the Great by Count Rastrelli, particularly, which is perhaps significant, in his own death mask. His moustache, and his general bearing, were modelled on Peter the Great.*

Diaghilev belonged to the county aristocracy, his father having been an officer in the *Chevaliers-Gardes*, one of the two Russian Household Regiments, corresponding to our Life Guards and Royal Horse Guards. His mother died when giving him birth. Later, his father left the regiment owing to his debts, remarried, and in 1882 when Diaghilev was ten years old took his family to live on the paternal estate of 'Bikbarda', a property of some forty thousand acres, with two country houses and a family mansion in the provincial capital, which was Perm. It is important to state his origins, for by no misconception could

* Serge de Diaghilev's mother was descended from the famous family of the Rumianzovs. One of Prince Rumianzov's sons, then an aide-de-camp to Peter the Great, bore an exact resemblance to the Tsar and is conjectured to have been his son.

Diaghilev have come from any other background. His was an old family of the Moscow aristocracy, used to the social life of St. Petersburg, but during Diaghilev's later childhood living temporarily on the family estates at Perm. And now let us consider Perm. In order to get there, at that time, in the eighties of last century, from St. Petersburg, for Perm was not upon the railway line, you had to travel by rail to Moscow, and thence to Nijni-Novgorod. You then went down the Volga on a river steamer for four days, and at the famous old city of Kazan you branched off on the Kama river, arriving, eventually, at Perm. It was less than a hundred miles from the Ural Mountains, and therefore from the frontier with Siberia. In fact, Perm was nearly in Asia. We repeat that neither Perm, nor Kazan, was on the railway line. My old edition of Murray's *Handbook to Russia*, 1875 edition, says "from Perm the only mode of travelling is by post-horse." Yet, it was a centre of provincial civilization. My guide book continues: "*Hotels:* Petrof's; restaurant very good; Nobility Club House, rooms very decent and moderate; Birjevaya, new and good." The home of the Diaghilevs, with their devotion to music "made an Athens of this provincial town of Perm." In 1890, when he was eighteen, Diaghilev came back to St. Petersburg, but the impressionable years of his childhood were spent in the near-Tartar city of Perm. It was the mixture of Perm with St. Petersburg that gave Diaghilev his character. A photograph of him with his two step-brothers, taken when he was about ten years old, and easily to be recognized even at that age, shows him in a Russian shirt and long Russian boots. I have often fancied that the Russian family in *La Boutique Fantasque* was a reminiscence of his childhood. You could not talk to him for long without wondering about his early days, far enough away in all conscience in St. Petersburg, but more distant still when you thought of Nijni-Novgorod and Kazan. I remember Diaghilev speaking of the marvels of the great fair, and of those two Tartar towns.

The most fantastic proof of Diaghilev's energy, and a feat worthy of his mythical forebear Peter the Great, was his summer season of 1919 at the Alhambra Theatre, opening on 30 April, only a month after the previous season had ended at the Coliseum. *L'Oiseau de Feu* was revived, and there was a sensational revival of *Petrouchka*. Now, at last, it was possible to hear Stravinsky. I knew the music of Balakirev's *Thamar* well enough to notice the parallel between its opening bars and those of *l'Oiseau de Feu*. But how beautiful is, and always will be, Stravinsky's treatment of the Russian themes in *l'Oiseau de Feu*! As for *Petrouchka*, this is no less than a masterpiece of theatrical music in the Russian idiom, and how curious to know that some of its hurdygurdy tunes were heard at the October fair in Munich! By alchemy they have become completely Russian. But the sensation of the season was the *première* of *La Boutique Fantasque* on 5 June, followed by the *première* of *Le Tricorne* on 22 July. I was by now at Balliol College, Oxford, and so missed the first performance of *La Boutique Fantasque*, though I saw it the second night it was given. André Derain's curtain with its palm tree in a tub and the huge 'cello in the corner, the man in spotted stockings and kneebreeches playing a guitar, and the dancer in pantaloons holding a masque, all these were effects altogether new in the theatre, bringing a new kind of painting to the stage. Also, this curtain matched in some extraordinary way with the piece by Rossini that had been taken for the overture. No less sensational were the horse-hair sofas and armchairs painted upon the wings, and the still lives of flowers above them, wonderfully simplified in effect. Derain's backcloth, we were told, was intended for the harbour of Nice in 1865, with an early paddle steamer in the foreground, and a few houses reduced to simple cubes of colour. But the whole effect was beautifully Mediterranean with its hills and tufted trees.

The music for *La Boutique Fantasque*, Diaghilev kept as a close secret, carrying the book about with him and not letting it get even for a moment into anyone else's hands. It was a collection of little piano pieces, written by Rossini for his own amusement in his old age, and the manuscript had reposed for years in the museum at his birthplace, the Adriatic town of Pesaro. Diaghilev was particularly pleased to find among these pieces a little Russian march, or *Kosatchok*, which the aged Rossini might have written specially for him. The theme of *La Boutique Fantasque*, it is perhaps not generally known, is an old German one, *Die Puppenfee*. There have been many attempts to make it into a ballet, and drawings are in existence by Bakst who had this idea in mind. But the ingenuity of Diaghilev lay in tracking down those little pieces of music by Rossini that so fitted it, and in giving to Derain the costumes and the *décor*. At the time, I used to regard the orchestration of these *Péchés de Vieillesse*, as Rossini termed them, as most masterly in treatment, but having later heard many of them played on the piano by Soulima Stravinsky I realize they are more amusing still in their original form and that Respighi to some little extent altered them about and destroyed their meaning. Also, there were more than a hundred pieces to choose from, and it is by no means certain that he chose the best. So often did I see *La Boutique Fantasque*, and particularly during the winter season of the same year at the Empire Theatre, that I am the victim of a curious hallucination or delusion concerning it, for I have only to hear the music of that moment when the can-can dancer reappears on the shoulder of her partner and after a dance on her points is carried off stage by the corps-de-ballet and the Cossacks—I have only to hear this music—and that means I have only to sing or hum it over to myself—and I am, at once, in the stalls or promenade at the Empire or Alhambra on some evening in 1919 surrounded by persons I remember, and with the younger shade of Mr. Cyril Beaumont, with redder hair, not far away, for he, too, was always there. I am indeed sorry that I missed the first night of the revival of *La Boutique Fantasque*, thirty years later at Covent Garden, with Massine and Moira Shearer!

In 1919 there were persons still living, including the veteran pianist François Planté, who had been guests at Rossini's parties in his apartment at the corner of the Chaussée d'Antin and the Boulevard des Italiens, in Paris; and I have often wondered if any of his guests ever heard *La Boutique Fantasque* fifty years later. *The Barber of Seville* had been written fifty years before that, and it was Rossini who said that one of his reasons for giving up composing music after *William Tell* in 1830 was because of the dearth of properly trained singers, it having been the retired *castrati* singers of a previous generation who in their retirement opened schools and were the best singing teachers. It is a thought that takes us very far back into the early 18th century! When seeing *La Boutique Fantasque* I was never able to forget that Nice, or at any rate that part of the Riviera which is the scene of it, was Italian in 1858. The old shopkeeper, so beautifully played by Cecchetti, was surely Italian; and I think that Diaghilev must also have been influenced by memories of San Remo, visited by so many wealthy Russians, years ago, and where there is still a Russian church with golden onion domes. The inclusion of Rossini's once famous tarantella into the music of *La Boutique* was most apt. It had been as popular in its day as *Funiculi, funiculá* and is a living relic of the Kingdom of the Two Sicilies.* But perhaps the most remarkable feature of all about this ballet was the ability of scene painters and costumiers to 'translate' the extremely simplified sketches of André Derain. His drawing for the backcloth was not much bigger than a postcard. Diaghilev had now completely metamorphosed his tastes, abandoning the world of fashion for that of modern painting.

The proof of this came six weeks later with the *première* of *Le Tricorne*. During this season of 1919 it was not to be forgotten that two of the great painters of the time were at work in London. I was taken to see Picasso at work on his drop curtain for *Le Tricorne* in a big studio near Leicester Square. The canvas was lying on the floor and Picasso and his scene painter were sitting on it eating their luncheon. Their bottle of wine stood upright just where the painted bottle and two glasses stand upon the tray. Having just returned from my first visit to Spain I saw in this drop curtain and in Picasso's costumes for the ballet a wonderful continuation of Goya's tapestry cartoons in the Prado. I was, then, intent on persuading my father to employ Picasso to paint frescoes in the *gran sala* of Montegufoni, his villa near Florence. Negotiations were entered into for this purpose, and in the autumn we saw Picasso in Paris and talked over the project. There were to be painted balconies over the doors, with Italian musicians, and big painted landscapes in the style, I hoped, of Benozzo Gozzoli; and Picasso, doubtless, had he wished, could have worked as close to Benozzo Gozzoli as he did to Goya. It was rage and disappointment over the frustration of this scheme that made me ill and gave me a nervous breakdown early in 1920. The ballet of *Le Tricorne* was the fruit of many months' study of Andalusian dancing by Massine. It still remains, if well performed, the best stage presentation of Spanish dancing, just as Massine in his *farruca* is without rival in the theatre. Even the most gifted of Spanish dancers, the superb Antonio, is for nocturnal entertainment on a stage in a café, or in a garden, but not in the theatre. The backcloth and wings of *Le Tricorne* in their simplicity were events of epoch-making importance in the theatre, and entirely new. It was the strange prerogative of Diaghilev to inspire painters and musicians and get results from them which they could not achieve, unaided. *Le Tricorne* is Picasso's best and only considerable stagework, as, also, it is the most popular work by de Falla. I

* At one time Bakst was to stage *Boutique Fantasque*, and says in a letter to Diaghilev: "I am comfortably busy working on the costumes for *La Boutique Fantasque*. It is to be a very resurrection of Naples in 1858." *Cf. Diaghilev*, by Serge Lifar, Putnam & Co., London, 1940. pp. 210–211.

remember hearing that Picasso sketched the design for the top of the sedan-chair from a pineapple in a bowl of fruit on a restaurant table in Soho. His dresses are no less than a wonderful, and original, repertoire of Spanish costumes. What could be more beautiful than the girls' dresses in the final *jota*, some in green and white, others in blue with eyes or *ocelli* in varying spots of black and white; or the glorious red and gold Torero-Harlequin in red and yellow with a cocked hat!

The autumn season at the Empire Theatre was notable for the revival of *Parade*, the ballet by Erik Satie and Jean Cocteau, for which Picasso drew a poster taken from the dress of the Chinese juggler, long used to advertise Diaghilev's seasons. *Parade* had, also, a drop cloth, now in an American museum, which is, all things considered, perhaps his masterpiece. It is a supper scene. The troop of comedians, a film-star, a Wild West character, a negro boxer, a child, and a Harlequin are at supper. The white circus horse, with wings, stands in the foreground pushing a striped ball along with its forefoot. A slanting ladder, and a colonnade complete this masterly design.

As though, not unnaturally, a little exhausted by his labours, Diaghilev's next season or two had fewer novelties to offer. There were difficulties as well, always financial troubles, Diaghilev having never more than enough money to pay his hotel bill. And, as well, there were difficulties with his dancers. Lopokova had left the company; and early in 1921 there was a quarrel with Massine as the result of which Diaghilev lost his choreographer. Meanwhile, the summer season of 1920 at Covent Garden had a ballet by Cimarosa with a setting by José-Maria Sert, and Stravinsky's *Le Rossignol*, for which Matisse designed the scenery and dresses, by no means his masterpiece. But there was, as well, *Pulcinella*, to music by Pergolesi which had been given a 'treatment' by Stravinsky, a carnival or fairground 'treatment'. Some of Picasso's alternative sketches for the scenery which were published in the souvenir programme were more interesting than the actual scene, as 'realized'. It had undergone too much simplification and become in the process like a caricature of Naples. Nevertheless, his drawings of Pulcinellas were inimitable and a companion series to his harlequins. As ever, they were his own conception, not to be mistaken for a moment for Domenico Tiepolo's great series of Venetian Pulcinellas. By now, I think it will have become clear that the accent was less on the dancing than on the music and the *mise-en-scène*. The supply of good dancers from Russia was running low, and the aim of Diaghilev was to amaze and astonish more than to satisfy. Jean Cocteau's influence was paramount with him, and *"maintenant, Jean, étonnez moi"* was the phrase he constantly used to Cocteau. Under those auspices he was drawn more and more towards the music of Les Six. The influence of Auric and Poulenc can be traced in the orchestration of *Pulcinella*, for it was to the Parisian public that Stravinsky and Diaghilev appealed as arbiters of taste. Of the London public they took little account, although the season ran three or four times longer in London than in Paris.

The summer season of 1921 at Princes Theatre had little new to show except *Chout*, an ugly ballet by Prokofiev, and new choreography by Massine to *Le Sacre du Printemps*.

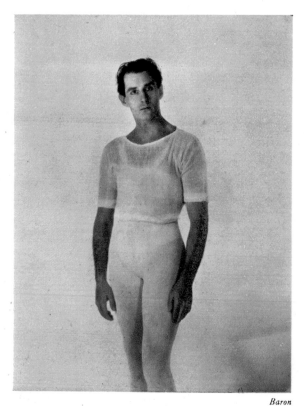

Anton Dolin

The *Sacre*, perhaps, had lost its force in the theatre and was better in the concert hall. Just before this, the music was performed in Queen's Hall with Eugene Goossens conducting, a memorable evening of noise and ordered turmoil, and I saw a young man sitting asleep in the row of seats in front of me. If he could sleep during such an uproar, I thought, he could equally have slept during the Battle of Waterloo, and immediately it was over I asked to be introduced to him. It was Robert Byron, who at once and on the spot became a friend of mine. But Diaghilev was only gathering his forces and his sensational return with a glittering galaxy of dancers took place at the Alhambra Theatre on 2 November 1921, the most exciting first night I have been to in my life. It was his revival of Tchaikowsky's *La Belle au Bois Dormant*, with Nijinska, Lopokova, Nemchinova, Spessiva as Princess Aurora, and as Carabosse, the wicked fairy, Carlotta Brianza, who had danced as Princess Aurora in the original production in St. Petersburg in 1890. English dancers in this wonderful list of names included Sokolova and Anton Dolin. I was at the Alhambra Theatre on most nights, and was present on 5 January 1922 when Cecchetti made his one appearance as Carabosse on the occasion of his jubilee. This was the rôle he had created in 1890. It was a classical demonstration of the old Italian art of mime, and no one who saw him on that evening will forget his exit in his mouse-drawn chariot into the wings. I was in the theatre, also, on the hundredth performance in the middle of January; and on the last night of all. The whole of this immense production, in five scenes with three hundred costumes, was miraculously achieved by Bakst within the short space of six weeks, although it is true that he had been thinking of it over many years. This was Bakst's last big production, and it exhausted him. The scenes in the style of Bibiena were a great novelty; the scenery and dresses, as a whole, not better than Oliver Messel's beautiful production at Covent Garden, with the exception of scene III, *The Vision*, a hunting-scene conceived by this great artist of the theatre in golden tones of autumn leaves. The Louis XIV hunting dresses of the Court Ladies were carried out in Bakst's favourite reds and oranges. This hunting-scene was in every way poetical and beautiful, and in natural relief, coming, as it did, between the scenes of statues and colonnades. The last scene of all, *The Awakening*, was in use for years afterwards as a setting for *Aurora's Wedding*, but by that time was much damaged from going on tour. Nothing like these Bibiena scenes had been put upon the stage before. Bakst, himself, seems to have fallen into disgrace with Diaghilev before the night of the first performance, and I remember seeing him sitting in the stage box at the Alhambra Theatre, on the right hand of the stage (now, like the Empire Theatre, a cinema) wearing a tweed suit instead of evening clothes, as though on purpose to signify his objection. It was the only time I ever saw Léon Bakst, but he was well known to me, if only from Jean Cocteau's caricatures. After this production at the Alhambra Theatre he spent most of his few remaining years, for he died in 1924, in the United States, where, last winter in Balti-

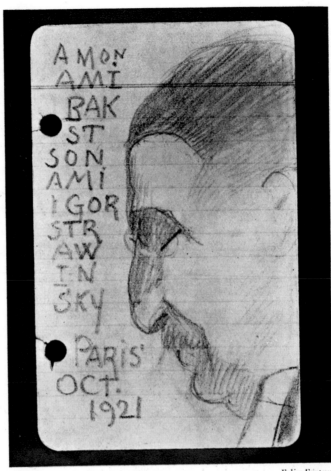

Felix Fonteyn

Léon Bakst by Igor Stravinsky

more, I was shown a theatre decorated by him in a private house. Rolled up in attics there were reputed to be several sets of scenery by his hand.

I had known every note of *La Belle au Bois Dormant* before, but now found new beauties which are eternal in it, for this is the masterpiece of Tchaikowsky and the music, of all music, for the classical dance. But the season of 1921-22 was a failure, and Diaghilev was nearly ruined by it, chiefly owing to the machinations of one music critic revenging himself at last on Diaghilev for his support of Stravinsky, and Diaghilev was driven out of London for two years. It was a mortal blow, and I do not think the Ballets Russes ever really recovered from it. To be assured of poor performances of Wagner at Covent Garden was no compensation for nearly destroying the great art movement of its time. It would be difficult to exaggerate the shock of surprise at the revival of *La Belle au Bois Dormant*. The whole evening was one long, unending succession of delights.* The entr'acte called

* Among them was the beautiful Maria d'Albaicín, as *Schéhérazade*, carried in a litter, to a languorous sham-Arabian air (actually the *Danse Arabe* from *Casse-Noisette* interpolated by Diaghilev into the score). Maria d'Albaicín was one of the most beautiful women I have ever seen in my life. It would be impossible to imagine a smoother skin or a more beautiful back and shoulders. She had been brought over

Panorama, played before a drop scene of a romantic castle, was overwhelming; and I have ever since thought that this entr'acte stands in relation to other music of the theatre as the slow movement of Schubert's quintet Op. 166 stands with regard to all other music, the most beautiful thing of its kind in the world, that is to say. Nijinska's *variation* as the Fairy of the Humming Birds was danced with extraordinary fire and brilliance. She had the pale, colourless hair of her brother and his slanting eyes, and resembled him, also, in the shape of her legs and movements of her hands. It was a most curious experience to hear again the music of this ballet when it was revived at Covent Garden on the opening night in February 1946 after the Second War had ended. I do not think Diaghilev would have been at all surprised to know that this Russian classic, now, a generation later is the most popular ballet in the world; nor that it would be permanently established in London and better performed here than anywhere else, for he always believed, and said, that there would be great dancers one day in England. However, not all his first night audience were of his opinion; Lytton Strachey told me that Tchaikowsky's music made him feel quite sick; while horror at it was expressed in as violent terms by someone else, all knowing, who is now literary critic of one of the Sunday papers. The memory, of course, is of a Russian performance of a Russian masterpiece: Russian, because of Diaghilev and Stravinsky, because of the slanting eyes of Nijinska, because of Bakst's whole conception which was nearer to the atmosphere of the Russian palaces, to Peterhov or Tsarskoe-Selo than to the legendary Versailles of Louis XIV; Russian, too, because of the terminations to all the dances and because of so many little details such as the negro guards of King Florestan, in reminiscence of the Court Arabs of the Tsar's palaces. It is this Russian atmosphere that must be kept in mind when performing *La Belle au Bois Dormant*, and it should never be allowed to lapse entirely.

The return of Diaghilev to the Coliseum in the winter of 1924 showed his partial recovery from the failure of two years before. His company included Nikitina, Dubrovska, Danilova, and Ninette de Valois. Two more Coliseum seasons followed, in token of reduced circumstances, yet he produced *Les Biches, Les Fâcheux, Les Matelots*, to music by Poulenc and by Auric; Boris Kochno now wrote his *libretti*, and Serge Lifar was his chief dancer. Balanchine was shortly to become his chief choreographer. He also produced in Monte Carlo three short operas by Gounod and one by Chabrier. Where myself was concerned there now began a period of closer association with him. The occasion of this was his wish to produce a ballet to music by Lord Berners, for which I was asked to write the *libretto*. I took Diaghilev to see paintings by Wyndham Lewis, by William Roberts, and by Edward Wadsworth, but Diaghilev was not satisfied. In the end I tried to explain to him what was meant by the 'penny plain and tuppeny coloured' prints of the Juvenile Drama, and took him down to see Mr. Benjamin Pollock in the old toy shop in Hoxton. The mass of

from Spain in the *Cuadro Flamenco*, a Gypsy entertainment imported by Diaghilev from Seville. Born in the caves of the Albaicín hill at Granada, and only seventeen years old at this time, María d'Albaicín could barely speak Spanish, and talked the Gypsy *caló*. To anyone who admired her, she would suggest that they would prefer her mother, who was, in fact, very beautiful and thirty-two years old. María d'Albaicín died of consumption before she was twenty years old, having given up dancing for film-work. She was one of the three most beautiful dancers the present writer has ever seen in his life upon the stage, and it is sad that she should be forgotten.

Gala Performance of 'The Sleeping Beauty' at the re-opening of the Royal Opera House, 20th February, 1946

material astonished him, but I do not think he ever understood what it was all about, or that Robert Cruikshank who designed many of the prints for H. J. Webb (the rival firm to Pollock) and his brother George Cruikshank were famous names, the latter of them in eternal association with Charles Dickens. He therefore produced *The Triumph of Neptune*, Lyceum Theatre, 3 December 1926, with an air of mystery where, really, nothing was more natural than a traditional English pantomime.

I must now as time is running short express my remaining impressions of Diaghilev in as short a space as possible. There was much opportunity of seeing him at work when I went to Florence in connection with *The Triumph of Neptune* in August 1926. Diaghilev was staying at a hotel on the left bank of the Arno, and the conferences took place in a huge room called the Sala di Santa Catarina, supposed once to have been St. Catherine of Siena's room. This was his bedroom. As always, intensely superstitious, he was horrified if anyone by mistake put his hat down on the bed. About these conferences there was a wonderful air of prodigality and a generous hand. When, looking at the Hoxton prints and making suggestions, I asked tentatively if we could have a pair of Harlequins in the ballet, he quadrupled the number and ordered eight. Most of his dancers were on holiday in Florence; he always insisted every year that they should spend a few days seeing the pictures and works of art in Florence and in Venice. We went with them to the Uffizi and Pitti Palaces, and to San Miniato where you look down on Florence, and he pointed out to them the tower of the Palazzo Vecchio and the Duomo. He also came out with me to Montegufoni, and we dined several times under a pergola at Fiesole, in company with Lifar, Balanchine and Boris Kochno. At work in the Sala di Santa Catarina, while Balanchine played the piano, Diaghilev drew up his plan of campaign, *danse générale, pas de deux*, and so forth, and it was a fascination to watch the workings of his mind. Later I saw him in Venice, where he stayed at the Lido, and would sit at Florian's, the café in the Piazza San Marco which had never closed night and day since the 18th century, drinking 'Americanos', his favourite drink, and never smoking. I often dined with him at the Vaporetto. It was ever an inspiration to watch Diaghilev ordering luncheon or dinner. He would screw in his monocle and look at the menu as though it was some enthralling ballet programme. At Kettner's, in Soho, where he often lunched, he had an arrangement whereby he had double helpings at single price. In the Savoy Grill Room he always occupied the same table, which has now his name inscribed under it in memory of him. My brother has recalled how Diaghilev who would never talk English, suddenly, one day at a luncheon in a private house, exclaimed "More Chocolate Pudding," to everyone's surprise. It was the only time I heard him speak a word of English. One of his characteristics was an intense and sincere love of physical beauty in both sexes and whenever he saw my wife, then a young girl of twenty, he would always come up and embrace her in the most

charming way. I would ask him all sorts of questions, eliciting from him that he had met Aubrey Beardsley at Dieppe in 1896, *"espéce de Jean,"* he would say of him, meaning that he reminded him of Jean Cocteau; and he also met Wilde during his last years in Paris. I asked him, too, about the first performance of *La Belle au Bois Dormant*, and he told me that he had met Tchaikowsky. He also talked to me about the great Anton Rubinstein, who was old when he heard him and had almost lost his memory. Rubinstein had, it seems, a marvellous 'entrance' when playing a concerto, and an altogether incredible sense of timing, and Diaghilev said that the famous 'entrance' at the beginning of Tchaikowsky's piano concerto, which was written for him, but never played by him, is, as it were, the portrait in music of this great pianist. Diaghilev had reached a stage in his career when he thought a safe road to success was the mating of opposites. I once suggested to him as a joke that he should put on a revival of *Schéhérazade*

Diaghilev at a rehearsal. Sketch by Christopher Wood

with dresses and scenery by Lord Berners, and I could see him considering the idea seriously, making, meanwhile, that chewing face which always meant that he was thinking. What was astonishing in him was his power of renewing himself and his ability to recover from disaster. When, owing to his quarrel with Massine he was left without a choreographer he remained three days in his hotel bedroom without food, and the first signs of his recovery was when huge trolleys of food were seen being wheeled into his room. For two days and nights before the *première* of *The Triumph of Neptune* he never slept, except perhaps for an hour or two in the early afternoon. He never went to bed at all the night before, and was in the theatre until after midday on the day of the performance seeing to the lighting. Much of the night he had spent helping Prince Shervashidze to paint the scenery, and himself, painting spangles on the transformation scene. Yet, that evening, he arrived in the theatre immaculate as ever, in full evening clothes.

During the succeeding seasons until he died in August 1929 I used always to go round to the theatre, as soon as I knew that Diaghilev had arrived in London, and would soon be helping him with some small job or other, more often than not with the choosing of his Symphonic Interludes.* I attended every rehearsal I could,† and had a free pass, often being allowed by Mr. Wollheim, his manager, to sit in the stage box. Somewhere not far away would be Diaghilev's old cousin Pavel Koribut-Kubitovitch, in evening clothes, looking like a retired ambassador, and who led the clapping. This delightful old gentleman with the difficult name had a way of applauding which, alone, could recall any dancer in front of the curtain for renewed applause. Diaghilev attended the performance of *Façade* at the Chenil Galleries and much admired the music of Walton, though he detected a strain of Elgar in him. He had discussed many other schemes with me for English ballets. Several times he visited Mrs. Gordon Woodhouse to hear her play the music of the Elizabethan composers, particularly John Bull, but came regretfully to the conclusion that their music was too old and slow moving and could not for that reason be made into a ballet. He was, also, interested in my schemes to make a ballet from Rowlandson's drawings, and Wyndham Lewis once painted on the wall of his studio somewhere off Church Street, Kensington, a wonderful satiric mask in the style of Dr. Syntax, with this idea in mind. This painting is probably still under the plaster on the studio wall, and may be found again some day. Diaghilev was, also, at Constant Lambert's instigation much interested in the music of Thomas Roseingrave, the English pupil of Domenico Scarlatti. This unfortunate musician, who was for a time organist at St. George's, Hanover Square, went off his head owing to an unhappy love affair, and composed music which was said to

---

* These Symphonic Interludes, an interesting study in themselves as showing the wide range of Diaghilev's musical interests and enthusiasms, were the means of hearing for the first time such pieces of music as Gounod's *Little Symphony for Wind Instruments*, Chabrier's *Minuet Pompeux* and the *Fête-Polonaise* from *Le Roi Malgré Lui*, Glinka's *Jota Aragonesa*, the finale from Balakirev's *First Symphony*, the *Scherzo in B* by Moussorgsky, *Islamey* by Balakirev, the *Gymnopédies* by Erik Satie, Rossini's overture to *Signor Bruschino*, Walton's *Façade* and *Portsmouth Point*, Bizet's *Jeux d'Enfants*, Dargomijsky's *Kosatchok*, various *overtures* by Méhul, and the *overture* to *Le Serpent a Plumes* by Delibes, a particular favourite with Diaghilev. He planned at one time to give a special season of early comic operas by Delibes, including his *l'Omelette à la Follembuche*. Delibes' one act comic operas were written at great speed for performance during the last years of the Second Empire, and there is no doubt that some of the most charming music of the composer of *Coppélia* and *Sylvia* lies hidden in them.

† It was amusing to hear Diaghilev singing at rehearsals. He would hum "Nitchni Nitchni Da Da Da," and so on.

reflect his madness. It was this that interested Diaghilev, and I received a long dictated letter from him on this subject when I was spending a winter at Amalfi. Another time I took Diaghilev to see a beautiful series of twelve fashion plates by Robert Cruikshank which were at Messrs. Sotheran, the booksellers. These were issued between 1820 and 1837 by a tailor, B. Read, of Bloomsbury, and are unique of their kind. The original drawings are in the Bethnal Green Museum. One of them depicts Brighton with its Regency bow-windows, and William IV riding in the street. Others show the new terraces in Regent's Park, and there is one showing skaters on the lake in front of Sussex Terrace with its domed towers. The proposal was that these fashion plates should be recreated by Rex Whistler. Incongruity, as I have said, then appealed to Diaghilev who had now reached the stage social hostesses have attained when they no longer ask persons to their parties who will get on well together, but collect them together on the particular assumption that they will disagree and 'make the party'. As an example of what I mean, there is little doubt that Diaghilev would have delighted in a performance of *The Marriage of Figaro* with dresses and scenery by Burne-Jones.

When his last season began at Covent Garden in 1929 it was noticed by his friends that Diaghilev looked ill. Personally, I had always hoped he would live to be seventy. He had talked of going to live in Taormina when he had to retire. But he had left London before the end of his season, and in only a very few days the papers announced that he had died in Venice on 19 August. His death was due to diabetes, and he was only fifty-seven years old. At his death the whole of the world he had created fell to pieces, and it seemed impossible that even the smallest fragments of it would ever come together again. During his last years it is true that he was more interested in book collecting than in the ballet, and I took him round the London bookshops on several occasions.* He was building up a library of Russian books, one of his particular interests being the books printed for Prince Antioch Cantemir. He collected, also, first editions of Pushkin. I said to him, once, "How good a writer is Pushkin?" And he replied "As great as Shakespeare." I have written so much about Diaghilev here, hoping it will interest readers, because 1954 was the twenty-fifth anniversary of his death. Celebrations in honour of his memory were held at the Edinburgh Festival and the successful exhibition there later moved to London.

The standard of dancing had much declined during his last seasons. There was nothing to compare with the dancing we were to see a few years later when Toumanova and Baronova made their appearance, the first products of the new schools of Paris. Even so, the young Markova, still a child, was in the company, and so were Sokolova and Danilova. But the corps-de-ballet were badly disciplined. At the time of his death, the next ballet to

---

* It was probably in search of Russian books that he paid a visit to Poland in the last years of his life. He went to Vilna, on purpose because it was unspoilt, and life there was as it had been in Russia fifty or sixty years before. I have very distinct memories of Diaghilev talking about the tour he made all over Russia during the winter of 1904–5 in search of portraits by Levitzky for the exhibition he was organizing in the Tauride Palace in St. Petersburg. There were three thousand portraits by various painters, and in search of them Diaghilev had travelled thousands of *versts* in peasants' carts visiting provincial governors and old Palladian country houses lost in the huge forests. I remember his describing to me the Imperial Palace of Tsarskoe-Selo with closed shutters in the snow, and of the incredible wonders to be found in the Chinese Gallery of the Imperial Palace, I think it was, of Gatchina, lying undisturbed since the end of the 18th century. At the exhibition in the Tauride Palace, a most haunting impression was given by the hall devoted to the 'mad' Tsar Paul I, always painted with his crown to one side of his head, and with a mad expression in his eyes.

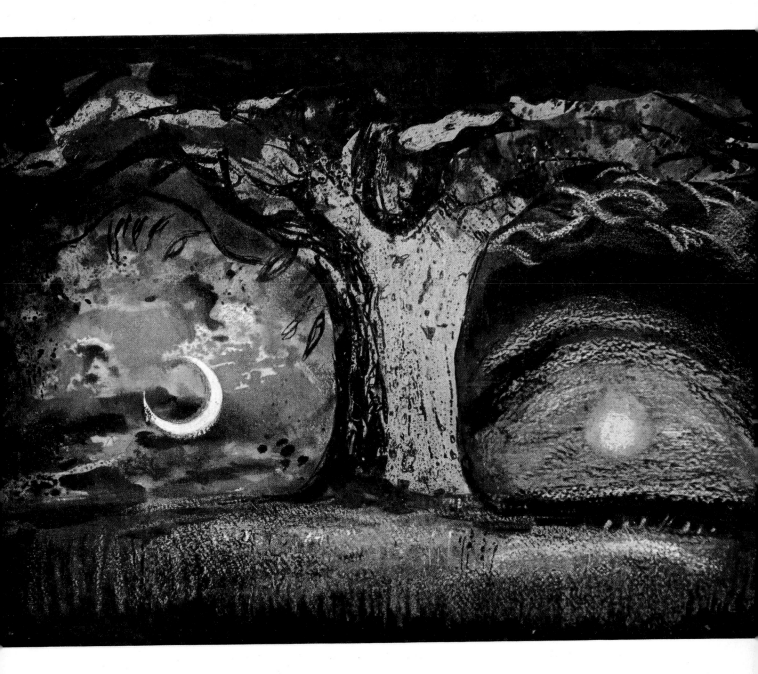

Job

John Piper's design. Covent Garden, 1948

be produced was to have been to music by Hindemith, in a setting by Cassandre, the French poster artist. As always, in these later years, the accent was more on the music and the setting than on the dancing. I certainly remember sitting in a stall at the Empire Theatre and the Alhambra, on various occasions, and wondering whether there would ever be an English company of dancers. In that day it was as unlikely as that there could be bull-fighters from England, or it could be said, for that is still improbable, cricketers from Spain. But the most unlikely things are contradicted and become true. That this should

have happened, and that the best dancers should now be English, is due entirely, as we all know, to the efforts of three or four persons, no more than that, these including Dame Ninette de Valois, Mme. Rambert, and the late Constant Lambert. The names of two great English dancers, Alicia Markova and Anton Dolin, must be mentioned too. It was Mme. Rambert, in her Mercury Theatre in Ladbroke Grove, who first gave our leading English choreographer Frederick Ashton his chance. For twenty-five years she has never failed to produce a succession of good dancers. And for a time after Diaghilev's death her little theatre was the only place in England where dancing could be seen. A particular kind of intimate ballet was devised for it by Frederick Ashton, making the most of its limitations of expense and space, and it was here that Pearl Argyle could be seen in little ballets like *Mermaid* and *The Lady of Shalott*, also in *Bar—aux Folies*

Houston Roger

Markova in ' Giselle,' Act I, the mad scene. Covent Garden, 1953

Bergères and other ballets. She was of transcendental beauty, her repose and modesty only making her tranquil loveliness more poetical and touching. She should always be remembered as one of the first and most beautiful of English dancers, with a talent particularly suited for the small theatre.

But, even by 1932, the beginnings of English ballet were laid on sound principles. The Camargo Society was in being. It was in the following year that Colonel de Basil gathered together some of the finest talent left over from Diaghilev's company, and with new dancers, as well, and with Massine as choreographer, produced the great 'symphonic ballets' to music by Tchaikowsky, Brahms, Beethoven, and Berlioz, perhaps disputable as works of art, but proving that there was a growing public and a future for the art of dancing. The beginnings of the Sadler's Wells Ballet date, too, from just this time, actually from 1931 when a group of dancers became permanently attached to the Opera Company at Sadler's Wells.

There is no space here, nor is there reason, to enter into full details of subsequent history. But the most exciting moment in the story of ballet in England was the opening night when the Sadler's Wells Company appeared at the Royal Opera House, Covent Garden, in February 1946, when the War had ended. By some magical means the Company, in spite of difficulties, had continued their performances all through the War. But this move to Covent Garden meant their removal to a larger stage and into full competition with the dancers of the world. Ninette de Valois, who had her training in Diaghilev's

Pearl Argyle

company, will for ever and always be associated with this great upsurgence and opportunity for talent. Robert Helpmann was the leading dancer, and his name, too, has already passed into theatrical history, while he is, in fact, making another career for himself upon the stage. Frederick Ashton returned to Covent Garden as choreographer and artistic adviser; and it could be said that the advice and musical experience of Constant Lambert were so invaluable that it is doubtful if the Company would have survived without him. When thinking of him, it would be well to remember that so much work as conductor and musical adviser may have to some extent stultified his other talents. It gave him little time for other work, and all his energies went into Sadler's Wells, and later, Covent Garden. But the revelation of that opening night was the dancing of Margot Fonteyn, and the realization that in her there was a *prima ballerina assoluta* of English birth and upbringing. Even so, it is true to say that she has improved even upon herself in more recent years and brought her talents to yet higher perfection. A *début* of astonishing promise was that of Moira Shearer, made a few days later, when for many of the audience her matchless grace and beauty were first revealed upon the stage. It was an experience to watch this young girl of twenty with her Northern colouring in the act of tackling the formidable, hair-raising difficulties of the classic dance. Since then, other dancers have come up to shine in the false sunlight of the stage, but none to equal these two who glittered in different intensity in the first weeks of that season. It is too much to expect that there should be new and good dancers every year. Two or three in a generation, and no more, has always been the rule. But it is a rate that can be accelerated with good training; and it is for this reason that the Sadler's Wells School is almost more important than the Company, itself. As soon as you have good dancers, the next thing to do is to worry about the dancers to come after them. They must be taken in hand at an early age and taught by the right methods. At the same time their other, ordinary education must not be neglected.

This present volume is published with just these ends in view. Our aim is to provide accommodation for a growing number of pupils. For the art of the dance is now established in England on firm foundations, and its civilizing influences are felt from end to end of the country. The status of the dancer is now such that it is envied in many other professions; but there is no other class of persons that works so hard and has to practise so incessantly, and it is important above all else that young dancers should have every care while they are children. There are countless numbers of the public who, like the writer, have derived some of the greatest pleasure and interest of their lives from ballet. Even now, the history of ballet in England has its ghosts and its traditions. Who, that loves such things, can walk down Charing Cross Road and not remember that Nijinski once crossed this road and went into that little and famous bookshop! It was Pavlova who said, often, that there would be great English dancers. In a shorter space of

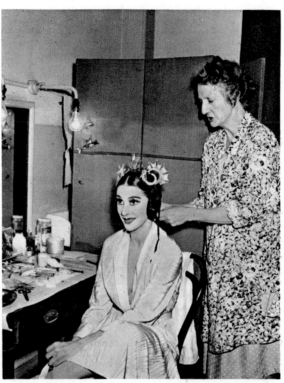

Felix Fonteyn

Margot Fonteyn and her dresser

time than anyone would have thought possible this has come to pass. The most hopeful sign of determination that this should continue is in the youthfulness of Her Royal Highness Princess Margaret, who is our patron. London is the home of the dance, and this is the School that may produce the dancers of the future. It is for lovers of ballet to look after their interests while they are children in order to applaud them when they fulfil their talents.

EARLY DAYS · 1931-1939

A Sadler's Wells Scrap Book with notes by William Chappell

Here we have Ninette de Valois as a peacock! 'Pride'— this little number was called — and it takes us back to the days when the repertoire at the Wells was so small that it had to be eked out with divertissments.
Take a look at that costume! One of the first I ever designed. That bathing dress bodice and cap look sadly functional. But take another look — and a good one — at those beautifully trained legs and feet.

Below — observe 'The Jackdaw and the Pigeons', an early work by De Valois. There she is, on the rostrum, in a pose that is still a typical feature of her choreography. This ballet had an all female cast, a sign of the times. Male British dancers were a very rare species in those days.

J. W. Debenham

John Baker

Ursula Moreton in (I think!) the first scene of 'Casse-Noisette'. She was, and is, a very handsome woman, and an invaluable aid to all unmusical dancers like myself. She would stand in the wings and count out the bars. I should never have arrived on the stage at all as Elihu in 'Job' without Ursula or Joy Newton to count me on.

Right is Elizabeth Miller in 'The Gods Go A-Begging'. Like many other early members of the Wells Company Elizabeth is now retired, married and a mother. In spite of all that I can't say she looks any different. A dancer's training is very preserving to the face and figure.

Gordon Anthony

Vaughan & Freeman

I haven't the faintest idea what De Valois is up to in the picture on the left! What an absolutely beastly bodice — but how well placed she is. Strong back, relaxed arms and hands and perfectly turned legs and feet.

On the right, De Valois as the tight rope walker in 'Douanes'. Her expression will be familiar to almost any dancer who has worked with her. It has that abstracted look which is likely to appear when a member of the company wishes to air a personal grievance!

Gordon Anthony

These two pictures are from the original production of 'Les Rendezvous', an early and still popular Ashton work. I was rather fond of the costume on the left — white and mauve — worn by Ailne Philips, but at that time nobody but me liked mauve! I have noticed it is considered rather an elegant colour nowadays.

Below, Markova and the legendary Idzikowski.

Markova was wonderful in this role, sharp, and quick as a wasp. And this was one of my best costumes. It looks quite horrible in this photograph but it was, in fact, very pretty; grey over blue, with black ribbons red roses and lilies of the valley.

J. W. Debenham

Above – Dolin,
Tudor and De Valois
in 'Douanes'.

On the right –
'The Jar', another
early De Valois
ballet.
Robert Helpmann
looks a bit like
little Bobbie
dressed up as Dad,
but Beatrice
Appleyard looks
ravishing. She was,
and is.

J. W. Debenham

J. W. Debenham

'Coppelia'. It's first production at the Wells. Stanley Judson (on the left) was the Company's first premier danseur. Here he partners Lopokova, and this is a

charming and typical picture of that small, round, delicious ballerina. In those days mime roles were played by members of the Opera Company. I can recognise John Greenwood on the extreme right.

This →
is the same production of 'Coppelia', with De Valois as Swanilda and Walter Gore as Frany. He is, I think, one of the most gifted dancers England has produced. De Valois' pizzicato feet were well suited to Swanilda.

J. W. Debenham

'The Haunted Ballroom', original production at the Wells. On the left Freda Bamford as Young Treginnis. Later, the child Fonteyn made her first solo appearance in this mime role. The ladies are Beatrice Appleyard, Markova and Ursula Moreton.

And here → is Ursula Moreton in 'Creation du Monde'. This Milhaud work was an early De Valois ballet, and a very difficult one. It couldn't have been very nice for Ursula when I danced the male role with her. She had to count ceaselessly to keep me on the off beat!

Mesdames Morter

J. W. Debenham

The first production of
'The Rake's Progress' was
probably the best. The original
Wells Company excelled at
the bawdy, especially
Sheila Macarthy, top, second
left, and Joy Newton.
They had a genuine squalid
gusto which no one else
has given to this ballet
since.

Left – Walter Gore and Markova
in the Bedlam scene.
I don't know why he has his
wig, shoes and shirt on.
He should not be wearing
them.

J. W. Debenham

Right — Harold Turner and
De Valois in 'Barabau'. Do
you recognise the familiar
De Valois pose? This ballet
had one of the best decors
I remember — by Edward
Burra who also designed 'Rio
Grande'.
Below — I don't know why
Walter Gore and I look so
hostile. On the left Gore and
Appleyard, on the right Fonteyn
and myself. This was Fonteyn's
first solo dancing role (no
pointes) and I like to remember
I was her first partner.

J. W. Debenham

'The Gods Go
A-Begging'.
Pearl Argyle as the
Shepherdess, myself
as the Shepherd.
I am amazed by
my fat legs. They
look as strong as
Idzikowski's.
Alas! They were not.

Opposite page, Pearl Argyle.
Most ballerinas are able to give an impression of beauty on the stage.
Very few are as unquestionably beautiful as this dancer was. She had
a face of really breathtaking loveliness, combining a thousand classic
features — and by classic, I do not mean the cold regular perfection
of a Greek statue. She had the human qualities of beauty to be seen
in Botticelli's Primavera and Birth of Venus; in the Boucher
Pompadour; and the fabulous Nefertiti head. She died young — and
it is easy to believe the Gods loved her.

J. W. Debenham

J. W. Debenham

Above—Pamela May, Harold Turner and Joy Newton in the original production of 'The Gods Go A-Begging'. How charming, how _young_ they look. This really is springtime. I think it is the only picture in this scrapbook that makes me sigh and turn the mirrors to the wall.

Left—this photograph too, touches me. It shows Argyle and Fonteyn as they both appeared in the name part of 'Pomona', an early Ashton work.

'Les Patineurs' — Elizabeth Miller and Mary Horner.

J. W. Debenham

'Les Patineurs' — Fonteyn and Turner.

J. W. Debenham

J. W. Debenham

'Façade'—another non-stop Ashton work. Born 1940 and still going strong. It's always been a mystery to me, the Wells mania for re-designing ballets. John Armstrong's original decor had real wit, and where is that lovely

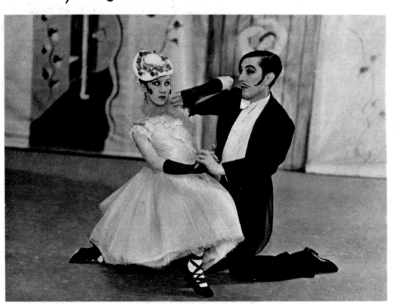

J. W. Debenham

melancholy cow looking out to sea? Above-the final group.

On the left— Ashton and Molly Braun in the 'Façade' Tango— a role originally danced with divine madness and ecstasy by

Lopokova. Ah—Molly Braun, where are you now? Retired, married, and, need I add?—a mother!

J. W. Debenham

'Façade' — old and new 'Waltyes'.
I still prefer the original costumes.
Above, June Brae, Peggy Melliss,
Pamela May and Beatrice
Appleyard.

On the night, I can only recognise
Gerd Larsen on the steps, right.
Oh dear — all these new faces!
I feel as old as Cecchetti.
The new dresses are too pretty and
refined for 'Façade.'

Edward Mandinian

'Façade'. Two Tangos.
Flame crowned Shearer with Ashton —
on the left. Raven haired Fonteyn
with Ashton – below.
There is only one Dago, Ashton. No other
dancer has his rich Southern subtlety,
his elaborate hands; his disgraceful
eyes — nor a quarter of his speed,
gusto and excitement.

This costume is
the only one I
would call an
improvement.
It's red velvet
draped hobble
skirt and tango
red shoes are
better suited
than the ballet
skirt and Dolly
Varden hat of
the original
production.

J. W. Debenham

De Valois as 'Webster' in 'The Wedding Bouquet'. The ballet that tore a muscle in my calf when I was summoned back, old and retired, for an anniversary performance in 1950.

The rehearsal period of the original production of this ballet was a link with the Diagileff world and the between wars period — brought back to us by Lord Berners and that ineffable pair, Gertrude Stein and Alice B. Toklas — with Constant Lambert — brilliant and lovable Constant in charge of the music & the frenetic libretto.

J. W. Debenham

On the right — 'Apparitions'. Ashton's first big romantic work. Masks, visions, laudanum, daggers, lilac and Gothic windows. Here is Helpmann in the cave scene. I <u>might</u> be one of the surrounding figures, but I cannot recognise myself upside down.

Cecil Beaton

53

Apotheosis!

Gordon Anthony

The first English production of 'The Sleeping Princess', Fonteyn and Helpmann in the centre. I'm afraid Aurora's Wedding was rather sparsley attended. It looks a little utility now — but it must be remembered that from this rose the glittering and gigantic child that is now an international celebrity. Goodbye — Dear Sadlers Wells — part of my youth. A formal bow to the Royal Opera House where I, alas, am but a foreigner in a strange land.

THE
SADLER'S WELLS
SCHOOL

Arnold L. Haskell

AS recently as fifteen years ago no ballet company could be safely applauded by the 'man-in-the-know' unless it bore the label *Russian*. It did not matter that on her passport, Lubov Smirnova was named Lily Jones, or that the exotic Xenia Petrova had been to an excellent girls' school in South Kensington, they were naturalized *Ballet Russe* and could pass in a crowd. In any case they were to be recognized rather by their Muscovite attire in the street than by their dancing on the stage.

Now this reaction—and it was mine—was part sense and part nonsense, part sound judgment and part prejudice. It all depended upon one's understanding of the words *Russian Ballet*, on a balanced understanding that had nothing to do with the glamour of the exotic. (And, let us admit that there is a great appeal about broken English. How well I remember our joy when an attractive ballerina told us, "my toeses is all bloodsome." We were her slaves; she could do no wrong.) *Russian Ballet* has a precise meaning, a scientific as well as an artistic meaning; it was Voltaire who said that he loved ballet because it was both a science and an art.

In the first place *Russian Ballet* meant the particular blend of the arts that had rescued ballet—it was usually called 'toe-dancing'—from the sterile prettiness of the Edwardian music-hall stage and had again interested the poet, painter and musician. Ballet's debt to Molière, Lully, Rameau, Boucher, Bérain had long been forgotten, as also to the more recent Théophile Gautier.

"I am a barman," Diaghilev once said, "and this *ballet russe* is my particular cocktail." He spoke the truth and his 'cocktail' was appreciated all over Western Europe. Only in Russia was it unknown.

What was not so clearly recognized was the other meaning of *Russian Ballet*, something equally important and something that truly belonged to Russia. It meant a definite *school* of dancing. Kchessinska, Trefilova, Pavlova, Karsavina, Nijinski, Spessivtseva were products of that school. Its ingredients were known and could be analysed. It came from a blend of the French and Italian schools, brought to Russia by Petipa, Johannsen, Cecchetti and others before them. The Russia of those days was, artistically speaking, the least chauvinistic of countries, and made no claim to have invented ballet. The Russian *school* was a system as well as a building—to be more exact, buildings in St. Petersburg, Moscow and Warsaw. Karsavina has written of the great St. Petersburg school [in both senses] in [her classic] *Theatre Street.*

It is this conception of school not merely as a building but as a system of education and a way of thinking that it is vital to understand. It is the foundation of ballet, without it there can be nothing but a jumbled acrobatic entertainment as insensitive as an orchestra full of substitutes. A national ballet cannot be made by gathering together the most promising dancers from a number of schools. This is particularly the case in England, where the tradition is new, and where there are endless private schools, many of which teach a different system.

The first problem of a national ballet was to create a truly English* style, a style that naturally derives from the great European traditions, but that is expressive of the national temperament. There is always a great deal of loose talk about dancing as an international language; in a sense this may be a truism, but it needs a considerable amount of explanation. Dancing is only interesting and only possesses integrity, when it is the expression of a nation's psychology. Russian dancing owes everything to France and Italy, yet is truly Russian. In the same way our own dance which is now rapidly developing along a line of its own, must always acknowledge its indebtedness to the Russian style. So definite is this question of nationality in dancing, that all too often, the public rejects dancing as bad when it does not conform to the style to which it has become accustomed. This very fact of the adaptability of ballet technique to every climate —the French school, founded by Louis XIV in 1672, the Russian school founded by the Empress Anne, the great school of Milan, the Royal Danish school, and now our own National School (of Sadler's Wells) founded by Ninette de Valois in 1931—shows its extraordinary strength, and its validity as a medium.

Felix Fonteyn

The first poster of the Russian Ballet, by Valentin Serov, representing Pavlova in ' Les Sylphides,' 1909.

THÉATRE DU CHATELET
SAISON RUSSE MAI JUIN 1909
OPÉRA ET BALLET

* I realize that the English style has been perfected by an Irishwoman and danced by representatives of the whole British Empire but I refuse to talk of a Commonwealth school!

II
SCHOOL IN PARTICULAR

Ninette de Valois started company and school together. She already had a nucleus to work upon, a group of enthusiastic pioneers who had been with her at her own private academy. She has written in the Sadler's Wells Gala 21st Anniversary programme of the scepticism of friends and well-wishers when she went to work in a theatre that was definitely on the wrong, the unfashionable, side of the river. The great inducement to work there, right bank or wrong bank, was the possibility of having a school attached to the theatre, of founding an English school of dancing.

The fact of having Alicia Markova as first ballerina of the company was invaluable from the school point of view. It made it possible from the very start to revive the Petipa classics. These classics are the great school pieces, for audience as well as for dancers. Ninette de Valois was herself a classical dancer of great brilliance but when she was dancing with Diaghilev there had been little scope. *Aurora's Wedding* was all that remained of *The Sleeping Princess*, the Alhambra production of 1921 that was intended as the start of a great classical revival.

Sergeeff's meticulous records of the classics, and Markova to shine in them, together with Ninette de

Michael Fokine by Valentin Serov

Valois' experience of production in the dramatic theatre, gained at the Abbey Theatre, Dublin, and the Festival Theatre, Cambridge, were a solid foundation for a school. The two were complementary; the English school had as its cornerstones the extremes of *Job* and *The Swan Lake*. It had in Frederick Ashton a choreographer who never mistook eccentricity for originality, who had the personality to create within the main tradition without losing his identity. He developed the company's artistry and he grew with it. It had Constant Lambert to guide it in musicianship. The last of the Russian discoveries, he was the first of the English. His compositions, his arrangements and his conducting are a part of our school.

Ballet is essentially an art of tradition. Camargo, Sallé, Guimard, Taglioni, Elssler, Zucchi, Pavlova, are not merely legendary names; they are all present on the stage today; Noverre, Vigano, Blasis, Cecchetti, Bournonville, Johannsen, Legat, Fokine have each made a positive contribution to style and to choreography. Their work is living, it can be pin-pointed. The great teacher of dancers must be in the direct tradition and must have had experience in the main stream of ballet. Should some crazy dictator ban the art for twenty-five years it would be lost for ever.

Here then is an important and interesting family tree. It could have been set out with many variations and naturally it lays no claim to being exclusive.

PIERRE BEAUCHAMP (1639–1705)
(Dancer and maître de ballet at the Académie Royale, Paris. He named the five positions, 1700)
|
LOUIS PÉCOURT (1655–1729)
|
LOUIS DUPRÉ (Le Grand) (1679–1774)
|
JEAN-GEORGES NOVERRE (1727–1809)
(Creator of ballet in its modern sense)
|
DAUBERVAL (1742–1806)
and
GARDEL (1758–1850)
|
CARLO BLASIS (1797–1878)
(Codifier of the classic dance)
|
GIOVANNI LEPRI
|
ENRICO CECCHETTI (1850–1928)
|
NINETTE DE VALOIS
|
SADLER'S WELLS ORGANIZATION

Marie Rambert, to whom English ballet, in particular its choreography, owes so great a debt was also a pupil of Cecchetti and Frederick Ashton studied and began his distinguished career with her. Markova and Anton Dolin were both the pupils of Seraphine Astafieva who, at the Imperial School, was the pupil of Johannsen and Legat. They also studied with Cecchetti. This same link with the great tradition may be found in the United States, the other newcomer to ballet, through Balanchine via Vaganova and Johannsen.

III

A DREAM COME TRUE

It had always been the intention to house under one roof a ballet school and a school of general education. The need was obvious. Growing children cannot give of their best when they dance after a full day's schooling and a struggle across London in the rush hour. Obviously under such circumstances they leave school at the earliest possible moment to concentrate on dancing. The exceptional child may continue to educate herself, but for the most part dancing becomes a purely physical manifestation. I can remember many a mother saying to me, "She is going on the stage—as long as she can read a contract and add up her pay packet she will get by."

It is far more serious however for the child who has sacrificed everything for her dancing only to fail, as the majority must. In that case she is quite unfitted for any skilled work and will certainly find it very difficult to adapt herself to a non-theatre life. I have seen, and still see, many of these pathetic hangers-on to the fringes of ballet. With general education and ballet under one roof no such problem arises, and, most important of all, there need be no distinction made between work in the classroom and the dancing studio; both are education. And ballet is an admirable education, not only physical but of mind and character. It requires discipline, co-ordination and quick thinking; also, as anyone who understands the dance will testify, very real humility. One of the most striking things of all is the complete lack of self deception among the pupils; they know as well as we do where and how they fail, they know where the real talent lies and they are eager to acknowledge it with generosity and enthusiasm.

General education and vocational training are usually best kept apart. In ballet this is not possible because of the need to create an instrument, the body, upon which the dancer will play. The artist develops with maturity but the instrument must be made when the body is supple. Intensive training in ballet is only for the very chosen few who have the necessary physical and mental gifts. Those selected children lose nothing educationally; on the contrary, there is a positive gain, unless we think of education from a purely academic point of view.

This school, however, in spite of all the arguments in its favour, remained a dream for a very long time. The ballet only performed twice a week and there was no money available. It was discussed—I remember conversations with Lilian Baylis and Ninette de Valois in 1934—and somehow I had little doubt that sooner or later it would materialize. I was used to the rapid expansion of Lilian Baylis' empire and had, after a couple of years of scepticism, gained unlimited faith in Ninette de Valois' extraordinary gift for long-term planning, especially after my close, exciting and enjoyable association with a Russian Ballet that excelled in a brilliant series of improvisations that left it poorer season by season.

It took the war to give us the school and a vast public prepared to admit that the English could produce ballet and creative dancers; a fact that Diaghilev had always known. I have always felt that Ninette de Valois' greatest triumph was to conquer our own public.

The Sadler's Wells Foundation decided to invest all the war-time profits of the ballet in the school, an act of practical idealism in the true spirit of its founder. A building, the former Froebel Institute, was leased at 45, Colet Gardens.

The actual start of the whole venture came in the most casual manner, over the phone. George Chamberlain, Clerk to the Governors, read me a minute from their last meeting appointing me Director, gave me the address of the building. He told me where I could find the keys and asked me to engage a staff and open as soon as possible. It was as easy as that. I had never heard the words 'Burnham scale', and I was, like all parents, a little scared of schoolmistresses. On the other hand I was sick to death of brilliant and suicidal improvisation, did not like periodical criticism and had always been more interested in children and education than in anything else—I still wish we could have a kindergarten. I was given all the help I needed in Doris Thellusson, the school's first Secretary, and in George Chamberlain to whom the school owes so great a debt and I could draw on the vast experience of the late Mrs. L'Estrange Malone, the first Chairman of the Governors.

It took a year of intensive work to get the war-damaged building ready for occupation —it was the era of permits for everything—and to engage the necessary educational staff. I soon found that the typical 'schoolmarm' was as much a myth as the typical anything else, though among the seventy applicants I intervewed there were some cranks. One in particular I remember with joy; apart from her excellent qualifications she was an amateur snake-charmer, a guitarist and an occasional contributor to *The New Statesman*.

The problem from the dance point of view was a simpler one. There, I had only to listen to Ninette de Valois and to take over something that was already in a flourishing condition. The Principal of Dancing from the start has been Ailne Phillips who left in 1954 to become personal assistant to Dame Ninette de Valois. She has been succeeded by Ursula Moreton.

It is as difficult to find a great creative teacher as a ballerina and in ballet the dancer has never finished learning. The teacher requires not only extensive knowledge and an impeccable eye but also considerable stage experience and yet she must be a teacher by vocation and not just a dancer in retirement. Ailne Phillips has been with Ninette de Valois since the pioneer days. She has the gifts of a great teacher with a range that includes the raw beginner and the ballerina in the company classes that she takes. And so from the very first the problem that I most dreaded, the co-operation between dancing and educational staff, has proved no problem at all. Ailne Phillips, Ursula Moreton and the present head mistress, Miss McCutcheon, have always considered every child as an individual and dancing and schoolwork have fitted together as a whole, as they should when the aim is to develop an artist. The same attitude has been adopted by the whole staff.

IV

GROWING PAINS

The school opened on 29 September 1947. There was no ceremony and no publicity. It was an ordinary school day save for the fact that the Bishop of London, the School visitor, walked through the building and blessed the school at work. The only vivid recollection that I have of our opening day was of a small boy, evidently a pupil's brother, coming up to me and saying, "please, Sir, where do you keep the mothers in this building?"

We started with 55 children, all girls. It was only in April 1948 that we began the essential boys' department.

From the first the school has been divided into four main sections. The Junior School (that is, the educational school) which is both a primary and a grammar school since we

 take pupils at nine and they remain until they have sat for the General Certificate of Education. The Senior School (or Students) made up of our own sixteens and of boys and girls who have finished their education elsewhere but whose dancing is sufficiently advanced for them to join our classes. There are among these students a great number from the Dominions and from all over the world. We have had students from the Argentine, Brazil, Chile, Finland, Iceland, Sweden, France, Japan, Malaya and the United States.

The Junior School follows a full grammar school curriculum, which it is able to do by substituting an hour's dancing a day for the gym, games or dancing of the ordinary school. The dancing term begins before the full term after the long summer holidays.

The Senior School concentrates on dancing, the students walking on at times at Sadler's Wells and Covent Garden but doing two hours a day of general education with the emphasis on the arts and humanities. One might call it the 'dancing sixth'.

The other branches belong to what we call The Associate School. The Junior Associates are children between eight and nine who do their schooling elsewhere but who come to us for dancing in the late afternoon or on Saturday morning. This is a very good way for us to find out if they are the right type to enter the school proper.

The Senior Associates are those who take dancing only. They are usually older girls and boys.

Pupils are selected by *Audition*—I have long been looking for a word that will describe

*'Petit rat' and her mother by
Louis Legrand*

what is definitely a process of being seen and not heard. They do not perform a dance or any set piece and we prefer them, if young enough, never to have had any ballet lessons. They enter in groups of five or six, graded according to age, and are given a few simple exercises to copy. The expert eyes of Dame Ninette de Valois and her colleagues can soon pick out the possibles, and at that stage it is only a question of making out a case for giving the candidate a trial. The word artistry is never used (except by some doting parents) at that early age.

Once selected the candidate is very carefully examined by Miss Sparger, the physiotherapist who has received ballet training, and who has written what is the standard book on the anatomy of the dancer. She marks on a sheet anything that may give trouble and, if she is in any doubt, the child is sent to an orthopaedist before final acceptance. There are many hidden flaws that have nothing to do with health or beauty in the ordinary way but that would prevent a successful career in ballet. Some of these faults are cured by ballet training and some by special exercises but others would only be made worse, especially by point work which calls for a specialized foot.

After this overhaul the candidate is then given a small written examination, partly a test of knowledge, partly an intelligence test.

We have found out in practice that those below a certain level of intelligence, however perfect they may be physically, always fail in their dancing once the elementary stage has been passed. This does not mean that the dancer needs an academic type of mind but that she must have quick reflexes and perfect co-ordination. The idea of the dancer as beautiful but dumb is wide of the mark. I like to think that we have played our part in killing it.

The final scene of this long audition day is an interview between the parent, usually the mother—though dancers do on occasions have fathers—and the Director and Head Mistress, with the child present. This interview is part fact-finding and partly for the essential task of urging caution. And how greatly caution is needed in the difficult period that is to follow. The parent must realize that acceptance does not mean success and that there is much that may go wrong in the years that are to follow. It is always a case of 'so far, so good'.

The child may grow too tall, too fat or too broad. All sorts of things can happen from a dancing point of view; that is, to feet, knees, hips and back. "To get into the company," I always say, "is very much like getting a major Oxford or Cambridge scholarship from an ordinary school."

These things are not said to pour cold water on enthusiasm but because in order not to be cruel later on one must be realistic at once.

"Every pupil here is taken on a year's probation, but even that means nothing, because things can and do go wrong at any time. We are not going to disturb the pupil in the year before the General Certificate of Education, but we feel that we must at all times tell you the truth. You in your turn must not make your child feel that ballet is the only possible career and you must never use the word *failure*. I have seldom known any pupil fail through her own fault, it is always through some accident of physique. If she never reaches Covent Garden or Sadler's Wells, she has at least had a good education and plenty of healthy exercise. She has lost nothing."

That is the refrain repeated to every parent and followed up by frequent letters in the same vein. On the whole we have had splendid co-operation. In practically every case a child feels very definitely when things are not going well. The carefully graded technique of classical ballet is a wonderful corrective to self-deception. Hence the many competent ballet dancers and the many ridiculous 'modern' dancers.

From 1947 a Teacher's Summer Course has been held in the school annually. While this has nothing to do with the ordinary school year the school staff take part and some of the children demonstrate. Ninette de Valois, designer of the course, gives many of the classes and assists throughout.

This course is very important in the history of ballet. It means in the first place that there is a definite English method to teach, a proved system that has produced the dancers who have earned fame throughout the world. This is not the place to analyse the method. It has developed over the years after a close study of the French, Italian and Russian schools and of their application to the English temperament and physique. Through the Summer School this method is now disseminated throughout the world—in 1953 no fewer than eleven teachers visited us from the United States—and so enriches the great tradition of which it forms a part.

V

MILESTONES

A successful school has little history except for those closely connected with it and for them the terms pass so quickly, the routine carries them so swiftly through the years, that they are unconscious of it. Mary is in Class I; Mary makes her debut at Covent Garden. Joan also in Class I, seems less fortunate; she is now a probationer at Barts. At any rate we have taught her to stand on her feet. Mary and Joan grow up and so the time rushes by.

There are, however, certain milestones:

June 1948: The first pupil to pass School Certificate, as it then was, and to get into the company at Covent Garden; Valerie Taylor.

19 *September* 1951: The school is recognized by the Ministry of Education as an efficient Primary and Secondary school.

1 *March* 1951: Princess Margaret visits the school, watches the classes and stays to lunch. The Princess Margaret Room, and a signed photo above the place she sat commemorates this visit.

1954. The School Governors acquire a lease of White Lodge, Richmond Park, to house the junior school.

G. B. L. Wilson

The White Lodge, Richmond Park

Don Quixote

Front cloth design by Edward Burra. Covent Garden, 1950

VI

OUR PROBLEMS AND OUR NEEDS

We have learned, and are, I hope, still learning by trial and error. Thanks to the understanding and the sympathy of education authorities all over the country many problems that seemed serious have solved themselves.

The possibility that has now come of being able to take boarders in a house of beauty and historic associations has solved two of our major problems. We can now draw talent from far afield and by retaining the present premises and adding those next door we can house senior school and give rehearsal facilities and amenities to the company itself. We have had an inspiring start in providing these studios. Monsieur Victor Dandré, Pavlova's husband, has left a legacy of £2,000 for a memorial to his wife. Our new studios are to be a Pavlova memorial, associating her forever with the country in which she had made her home and with the English dancers whose talent she was the first to recognize in a practical manner. Our most urgent and immediate need now that our physical requirements have been so generously met is for an Endowment Fund. At the present moment no private school can exist without an endowment—and we have an expensive double staff and must take all the talent that we can find.

VII

The success of our efforts in the school will be the number of former pupils dancing in this great Gala Performance; but to me as the Director, that will not be the only sign of success. I like also to think of former pupils sitting in the auditorium, enjoying their evening all the more for the understanding they bring to it; hospital nurses, secretaries, university students, who can see ballet without a pang of regret and who will only remember the pleasure that they had in their schooling at Sadler's Wells.

'*On the way to class at the Opéra*' from the
engraving by Raynouard

The School

H.R.H. Princess Margaret visits Sadler's Wells School

(top) *After luncheon rest*

(bottom) *Pas de deux class taken by Harold Turner*

(opposite)

(top) *Boy students' class*

(bottom) *Dalcroze Eurhythmics*

Evening Standard

Felix Fonteyn

Felix Fonteyn

Felix Fonteyn

69

Felix Fonteyn

Evening Standard

Miss Ursula Moreton, Ballet Principal of Sadler's Wells School since September, 1953

opposite)

top) Students working in the Pearl Argyle Memorial Library

bottom) Lunchtime : the junior school

(overleaf) In the Classroom

(top) Geometry

(bottom) Biology

Evening Standard

In Conference : Miss Ailne Phillips, Ballet Principal, Mr. Arnold Haskell, Director, and Miss L. McCutcheon, Head Mistress

Felix Fonteyn

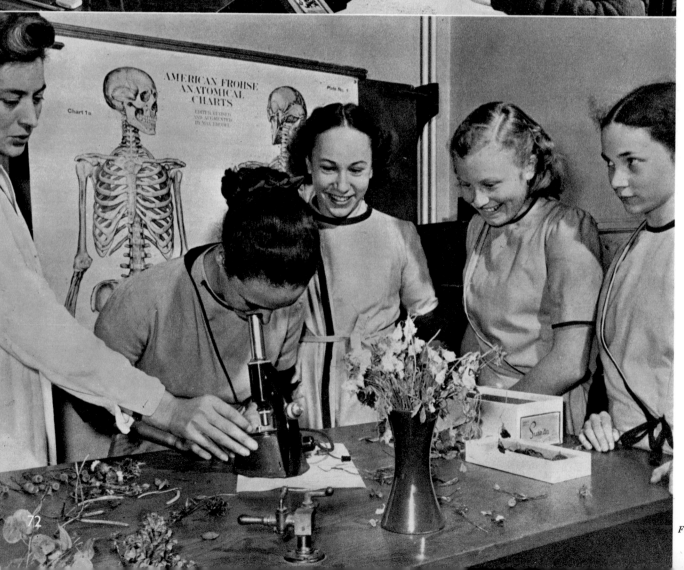

72

Felix Fonteyn

THE SADLER'S WELLS BALLET

James Monahan

OF the many occasions on which the Sadler's Wells Ballet has danced at Covent Garden, the stateliest, I suppose, have been the two Royal Command Performances in honour of a visiting French President. The first of these two was in the ominous spring of 1939 when war was but a few months away and when M. Lebrun was President; the second was when M. Vincent Auriol paid his state visit in 1950 and when the London 'atmosphere', if much less ominous, was also much more austere than it had been eleven years before. In 1939 the Sadler's Wells Ballet did not belong to the Royal Opera House. Its command performance, in that year, was an isolated adventure; the young company descended for a single evening from its relatively remote pastures in Islington and we, who had followed its infant career with proud anxiety, were particularly proud that it should have been thus honoured and, at the same time, particularly anxious lest it might not yet be of sufficient stature to justify the sudden compli-

Souvenir programme of the Gala Performance in honour of President and Madame Lebrun, designed by Rex Whistler

ment. The test was, indeed, unfairly hard. The Opera House that evening was magnificent; the audience was in the full gold and silver glory of court dress—no audience half so ornate has been seen in Covent Garden since then. The make-believe splendour on the stage could not, in fact, begin to compete with the display on this side of the footlights. The ballet was *The Sleeping Beauty*—a choice which, as I hope to indicate a little later, was significant. At the time, it seemed brave to the point of rashness. This, it should be remembered, was the company's first version of the famous classic, as dressed and decorated in rather modest style by Nadia Benois; it was not the new post-war production to which Oliver Messel gave costumes and décor and which was the first ballet seen at Covent Garden after the war.

It was quite different when, a decade later, M. Vincent Auriol paid his visit. By now, of course, the company had been resident in the Royal Opera House for some four years. Its choice as entertainer on a state occasion was no longer a surprise; on the contrary, it would have seemed odd had it not been chosen—such was its change of status since the visit of M. Lebrun. It should be added that in 1950 the company encountered a good deal less competition from the audience; this time mere evening dress was permitted and it was the audience which was comparatively drab. All the same, the company was able to put on a royal command performance of a class which was well beyond its capabilities a decade earlier, and I would mention one ballet in particular of those performed that evening—Frederick Ashton's *Symphonic Variations*—because, like *The Sleeping Beauty* eleven years earlier, it was, I consider, a significant, even, perhaps, a symbolic choice.

Indeed, if I have introduced these observations of mine on the Sadler's Wells company with a somewhat lengthy preface about these state occasions of 1939 and 1950, the reason is precisely that these two occasions serve so nicely as symbols or at least as milestones. For consider the point reached by the company in 1939. It was some eight years since Lilian Baylis and Ninette de Valois had brought it to life and some four years since Markova, the ballerina on whom the company at first so largely depended, had departed to start a company of her own. Thus, in 1939, the company was very young but, for four years, had already been obliged to show whether, without a prefabricated star, it could survive. As we know, it had proved not only its powers of endurance but also its ability to produce Margot Fonteyn—a ballerina of its own. She, of course, was the Aurora in *The Sleeping Beauty* of 1939.

Again, even if the pre-war production of this, the most exacting of the classics was, as it was bound to be, some way short of satisfactory, it was significant that the fledgeling company should be producing this ballet at all. No company had produced it in Western Europe since Diaghilev had done so, at the Princes Theatre in 1921 with such grandeur and at such financial loss. The Sadler's Wells repertory already included *Giselle, Casse Noisette, Swan Lake* and *Coppélia*; in adding *The Sleeping Beauty* to her company's stock of classics, Ninette de Valois, had, in effect, proclaimed that this company, for all its youth, considered itself to belong to the great tradition. It was using the classics—not a gingerly

[*continued on page* 87]

The Sadler's Wells Theatre Ballet
at Sadler's Wells Theatre

A Souvenir

Svetlana Beriosova and David Blair in 'Assembly Ball'

Roger Wood

75

Roger Wood

'*Khadra*,' *second edition, May 27th*
(*top*) *Sheila O'Reilly in the title roll*
(*bottom*) *General scene*

(*opposite*) '*Sea Change*'
(*top*) *David Poole as the Skipper*
(*below*) *Maryan Lane and Michel Hogan*

Roger Wood

'*Harlequin in April*'

(*top*) *Pierrot, Stanley Holden, Harlequin, David Blair and Columbine, Patricia Miller*

(*bottom*) *Entrance of the Unicorns*

Baron

Baron

78

Denis de Marney

'Blood Wedding'

(l.–r.) David Gill, Maurice Metliss, Elaine Fifield, David Poole and Pirmin Trecu

' *The Rake's Progress,*' *the orgy scene*

David Blair as the Rake, with Stella Clair the dancer

Ballabile

Original design for the front cloth by Antoni Clavé. Covent Garden, 1950

Denis de Marney

'*The Haunted Ballroom*'

(*l.–r.*) *Annette Page, David Poole, Joan Cadzow, Stella Clair and Yvonne Barnes*

'Pineapple Poll'
Elaine Fifield and David Blair

Baron

Scene 2.   Elaine Fifield and David Poole

Denis de Marne

82

Denis de Marney

'Coppelia'

Elaine Fifield as Swanilda and David Poole as Doctor Coppelius

'Coppelia'

Maryon Lane as Swanilda and Pirmin Trecu as Franz

Pirmin Trecu

Patricia Miller

In the rehearsal room at Sadler's Wells Theatre

*(l.–r.) Peggy Van Praagh, Frederick Ashton, Ursula Moreton
and Cecil Beaton looking at the costumes of ' Casse Noisette '*

selection of them but the complete list—as the foundation of its repertory, as the test of its dancers' classical technique and as the standard by which its own choreography should be judged. That, I suggest, is why this performance of *The Sleeping Beauty* at Covent Garden in 1939 might well be considered symbolic.

To say that the classics were the basis of the Sadler's Wells repertory in these pre-war years, does not, of course, mean that the repertory was exclusively classical. Two kinds of choreography, besides that of Petipa and Ivanov, are I think characteristic of the Sadler's Wells Ballet. Of one type Frederick Ashton is the principal master. He, it is true, had shown his choreographic versatility before the war and, with *Apparitions* and *Nocturne* had given broad hints of his mature and most memorable achievements. But his best work was not to come till after the war. Of the other modern type of choreography Ninette de Valois herself is the principal exponent; by 1939 her *The Rake's Progress* and *Job* had already given well nigh complete expression to this particular idiom. *Job*, indeed, was not a ballet born of Sadler's Wells; it was a little older than the company and might be described as one of the principal foundation members of its repertory. There are, admittedly, great stylistic differences between *Job* and *The Rake's Progress;* and *The Prospect Before Us*, which Ninette de Valois produced during the first year of the war and which belongs to the same choreographic family, is, in many ways, different from each of them. Yet it is, I think, the similarities of these three works which matter, rather than their differences. They are, of course, most obviously alike in being derived from pictures, but they are also ballets of complicated narrative, their choreographic techniques, though various, do at least share much freedom of expression and, above all, their themes are, all of them, extremely English—inspired by English pictures and set to English music. (It is not the first time that a Hibernian has proved more English than the English themselves.)

Of all Ninette de Valois' ballets *The Prospect Before Us* (specially as it used to be danced by that very funny man, Robert Helpmann) happens to be my favourite. For the moment, however, I am concerned not with my own or others' favourites but with what seem to me to be the most characteristic of the Sadler's Wells' works. So, again, I do not forget that Ninette de Valois has produced before, during and since the war, other ballets which are of a standard possibly as high as that of *Job*, *The Rake's Progress* or *The Prospect Before Us*. But these other ballets are not—or so it seems to me—so special to the manner and spirit of Sadler's Wells.

Here I allow myself a digression, though one which may not perhaps be wholly irrelevant. We know now that what mattered in ballet in Britain in the nineteen-thirties was the development of the young company in Islington. But the nineteen-thirties was also the period of the de Basil company, whose London reign, it may be remembered, began so brightly at the Alhambra in 1933 and was already ending in dreary internecine squabbles before war or the threat of war finally swept away its whole precarious structure. It was at the Alhambra in 1933 that I made my own belated discovery of ballet. And now not even the most generous use of hind-sight will permit me to convince myself that it was the 'Vic-Wells' in its very early spring-time, rather than the touring Russian ballet in its advanced autumnal days, which gave me balletomania. First impressions are the least forgettable. My first impressions of ballet were of Massine as the miller in *Tricorne*, of Massine, again, as the hussar and Baronova as 'the first hand' in *Beau Danube*—and, again, of Baronova with Lichine in the second movement of *Présages*. It was these performances—also those of Riabouchinska (*Choreartium*) Danilova (*Boutique Fantasque*), Verchinina (*Présages*), and Shabelevsky (*Les Matelots* and *Cotillon*)—which set my standard of dancing, just as it was the de Basil ballets—both the new works of Massine and Balanchine and the works inherited from Diaghilev—which set my standards of choreography and of production. People whose first ballet memories are of the Diaghilev company—even of his company as it was in the late 'twenties—were given standards of production, though probably not of dancing, higher than those provided by the de Basil company. However that may be, my debt to that company remains enormous—not least because it gave me a yardstick by which to measure the achievements of our own ballet. I wonder sometimes if a later generation—having seen neither Diaghilev nor de Basil—can so well measure the British ballet's achievement. (But, here, I realize, I begin to speak with the voice of old fogeyism.)

Quite apart, however, from such reflections, fogeyish or not, the de Basil company undoubtedly rendered a service to Sadler's Wells. It did this by maintaining—or, rather, by greatly increasing—the popularity which Diaghilev had won for ballet in this country. The de Basil company, in short, formed an invaluable bridge from the era of cosmopolitan, exiled-Russian ballet to that of national ballet. It would even be fair to say that but for the enormous popularity of the de Basil company shortly before the war, the Sadler's Wells Ballet would not have received all that popular support which helped it to survive so triumphantly the six difficult war years. That does not, of course, explain the whole of Ninette de Valois' and her company's astonishing essay in survival between 1939 and 1945; it is only a little part of the story but it is a part worth remembering.

I had mentioned (before this digression into the far-off de Basil days) that two of the most significant choreographic achievements of Sadler's Wells have been the revival of the classics and the invention (by Ninette de Valois) of the really English idiom in ballet. The latter achievement was already almost complete before the war; much, too, had been done by then towards the revival of the classics—though they were not performed altogether satisfactorily till the company, in the years after the war, had attained its new technical proficiency. The third of the company's most characteristic choreographic achievements is due—as I have also said—to Frederick Ashton. This, in effect, has been the development of a neo-classical style of choreography which is very distinctly related to the nineteenth century tradition of Petipa (so enormously appreciated by Ashton), owes a good deal to Balanchine (the only other comparable master of neo-classicism) and is, at the same time very personal to Ashton himself.

A mistake committed by all enthusiasts (forgivably in the young, less forgivably in the old), is to insist on the merits of one kind of ballet to the exclusion of all others. The plain fact, of course, is that unless programmes of ballet are to consist entirely of long three-act works, in the manner favoured by the classics and followed rigorously (and tediously, I feel) by the Soviet Russians, there must be variety in a company's choreography. We may prefer one kind of choreography to another but triple-bills (the normal rule in non-Soviet ballet) which do not contain variety, tend, obviously, to be boring—witness the dreary sameness of the programmes provided by a certain American company which is dominated by Balanchine's arid type of neo-classicism.

David Webster, General Administrator, The Royal Opera House, Covent Garden

Thus, if, for some imaginary or real gala performance by the Sadler's Wells dancers, an ideal programme were to be chosen—one in which the separate items could be at once most characteristic and most successful in their various ways—room would have to be found (at least in the programme of my choice) for *The Prospect Before Us*, and for, perhaps, the *Rose Adagio* or even for the whole of the very familiar second act of *Swan Lake*. There would, I know, be a great deal of squabbling over this programme. Some, for instance, would say that any selection of the most characteristic works must include Ashton's evergreen *Façade* or, perhaps, Robert Helpmann's *Miracle in the Gorbals* or even his *Adam Zero*. Some people would insist on a work by John Cranko—say, *Harlequin in April*—or perhaps Andrée Howard's charming *Assembly Ball*. I would be accommodating to all suggestions—except one; for I would not accept any suggestion that Frederick Ashton's *Symphonic Variations* might be omitted. In other post-war works by Ashton—*Tiresias* for instance, and *Daphnis and Chloe*—I find more and more to admire; and always what is most admirable is some passage, long or short, in which he has expressed his extraordinarily musical taste in neo-classical dance. But in *Symphonic Variations*, as in no other work, he has managed, so to say, to imbue a whole ballet with this neo-classical style of his—in a manner which has the apparent simplicity of true art. I know of no comparable achievement in modern ballet unless it be Fokine's *Sylphides* (before we saw it badly done for the two-hundredth time) or Balanchine's lovely, lost *Cotillon*. And such a work I take to be characteristic of our national ballet; it is at least a sign that this company has not only rediscovered the great European tradition but is also adding to it. I should add that John Cranko would seem to be the obvious heir to de Valois-Ashton-Helpmann as chief British choreographer and that his talent appears to lie, partly at least, in Ashton's neo-classical direction. Do I—in spite of my reminder that a ballet repertory must be various—show too pronounced a preference for neo-classical works? Perhaps I do. Only it should be remembered that it is dance, not drama or narrative or anything else, which is both the essence of ballet and its preservative. A ballet company needs many kinds of ballet but those which last longest are those which contain the most dance. Of this sort is *Symphonic Variations*.

If, then, the ballets chosen for this gala performance are to be at once particularly successful and particularly characteristic, the same criterion, no doubt, should apply to the chief performers as well. Here, however, I shall not try to select by name more than one dancer for the occasion—Margot Fonteyn, the indisputable ballerina. Beyond that, I would only say that, as it seems to me, the characteristic dancers of Sadler's Wells, those in whom is detectable an English style (distinct from, say, the more steely, athletic American style of Rosella Hightower or Maria Tallchief) are the lyrical dancers rather than the virtuosi. The characteristic Sadler's Wells dancer is an Odette rather than an Odile. Thus it is not hard to see whom I would regard as characteristic: Beryl Grey, Beriosova (both of them supremely so), Moira Shearer and (in a more junior class) Mary Drage. Margot Fonteyn, too, should certainly belong to this category—only she cannot really be confined within it; by temperament an Odette, she has taught herself to be an almost peerless Odile as well. Among uncharacteristic dancers I would place Violetta Elvin, Nadia Nerina, Rowena Jackson and, perhaps, Elaine Fifield. Since these are a rarity in this English company the need for them, on this gala occasion, would be all the greater.

To these lavish recommendations, however, I would add, finally, a note of astringency. Though I, personally, may have a weakness for the lyrical rather than the bravura style, for Ulanova and Fonteyn rather than for Lepeschinskaia and Hightower, this certainly does not mean that our national style—calm, aloof, elegant, long-limbed, as it tends to be, rather than vivacious, flashing, sturdy—is without its considerable limitations. Some American dancers, with their breath-taking technique, remind us occasionally of the nature of some of these limitations. A great Russian dancer (Ulanova, for instance) reminds us, still more effectively, that the Grand Manner is something which the great ballerinas must possess and which is not to be acquired by a national ballet, however good, of only twenty years of age. As with dancers, so with ballets: we do well to remember that, though our ballets may be instructive to the French, the Danes, and the Americans, nevertheless French ballet décor can often make English décor look frowsy, American ballet is rich, where ours is impoverished, in folk-lore and folk-dance, and the Danish ballet has joined an old tradition to an enviably youthful vivacity. For the sake of the future of our national ballet let us be grateful that the Sadler's Wells Ballet still has much to learn.

The Sadler's Wells Ballet
at Covent Garden

A Souvenir

Margot Fonteyn as The Firebird

Houston Roger

Houston Roger

Svetlana Beriosova as the Tsarevna

Houston Roger

Frederick Ashton as Kostchei, the immortal

The Firebird (Margot Fonteyn) casts her spell

Houston Rog

Wedding of the Prince and Tsarevna

Daphnis & Chloe

Sketches by John Craxton

Dorkon

Daphnis

Pirate

'Don Quixote'
Nadia Nerina and Alexander Grant

Roger Wood

'Ballabile'

Anne Negus and
Alexander Grant

Baron

97

'Ballet Imperial'

Roger Wood

Roger Wood

'Mirror For Witches'

99

'The Shadow'

Philip Chatfield, a youth, Svetlana Beriosova, his romantic love,
Brian Ashbridge, The Shadow

'Tiresias'

Margot Fonteyn as Tiresias

101

'Bonne Bouche'

Mother and daughter—Pamela May
and Pauline Clayden

Denis de Marney

Gilbert Vernon, the officer, Fiorella
Keane and June Lesley, his Past,
Pauline Clayden, his fiancée

Denis de Marney

102

Baron

'Donald of the Burthens'

Alexander Grant as Donald and Beryl Grey as Death

Baron

Richardby at Baron Studios

'Giselle,' Act II

'Giselle,' Act II

Roger Wood

'Daphnis and Chloe'

(above) Michael Somes

(left) Violetta Elvin and Michael Somes

(opposite) Margot Fonteyn and Michael Somes

Baron

Roger Wood

'Cinderella'

Beryl Grey as Winter

Moira Shearer as Cinderella

Roger Wood

' *Cinderella* '

The Prince's Ball—Act II, Moira Shearer and Michael Somes

'Sylvia'

Act III.   Aminta, Michael Somes and Sylvia, Margot Fonteyn

Sylvia

Robin and Christopher Ironside's design for Act III. Covent Garden, 1952

Overleaf: Scenes from ' Sylvia '

Brian Shaw and Peter Clegg

*Michael Somes, Alexander Grant
and John Hart*

'*Wedding Bouquet*'

Robert Helpmann, Moira Shearer, Margaret Dale

'*Dante Sonata*'
Michael Somes and Margot Fonteyn

Pamela May, Michael Somes and Margot Fonteyn

'*Apparitions,*' *Final Tableau*

Roger Woo

MUSIC
AND THE BALLET

Robert Irving

BEFORE embarking on a brief review of the general position of music and musicians in the world of the ballet, let us take a quick look at the musical side of the Sadler's Wells story. Here the horizon is naturally dominated by the imposing figure of that brilliant and fascinating character, the late Constant Lambert.

Lambert had an early introduction to the ballet, being commissioned to write *Pomona*, an elegant and charming work for small orchestra, for the Diaghilev company in 1927, when he was twenty-two. It was in the purlieus of the Russian ballet that he first met Ninette de Valois, and he had already made a big reputation as composer, especially of the dazzling *Rio Grande*, when he was later invited to become her musical director in the early days at Sadler's Wells Theatre. He was to prove the central tower of support as conductor, composer, and an adviser of incomparable acuteness, through all the years of development.

Apart from Lambert's expert musicianship, which contained that vital element of adventurousness and interest in 'lost' composers, he possessed that rare combination of creative force and a nimble and practical intelligence, which was ideal for the planning of a bold and varied musical policy. As a conductor, apart from his love of the ballet, he had that essential sense of movement, although he himself was physically handicapped by a severe illness as a child.

This sense of movement was conveyed in his beat, which seemed to include within itself the inner components of the rhythm, while never losing sight of the dramatic significance of the music, as it affected the action of the ballet. Finally his warm humanity and burning enthusiasm were exactly the qualities required for working with a theatre orchestra, whose members are not constantly buoyed up by the public acclaim of the concert platform, and consequently need more encouragement to retain faith in their jobs. He was most ably supported by the violinist Joseph Shadwick, who has similar virtues as leader of an opera orchestra.

A short glance at the repertoire of the pre-Covent Garden period will reveal Lambert's policy of mixing judiciously the three categories of music, established scores of a balletic or symphonic nature, adaptations or rearrangements of previously written music, and new scores commissioned from British composers.

In the first of these three classes, most important are of course the full-length classical ballets. These were gradually ushered into the repertoire, as the company grew in size and experience, starting with the two-act *Giselle* and *Casse Noisette*, the three-act *Coppélia*, *Lac des Cygnes*, and finally *The Sleeping Beauty* in 1938. More use was made initially of the shorter scores of the Diaghilev era, such as *Carnaval* and *Les Sylphides*. More adventurous were the new versions of Stravinsky's *Baiser de la Fée* and Milhaud's *Création du Monde*, and the brilliant orchestral version of Walton's *Façade*, which had received its balletic baptism in humbler guise. As regards the non-balletic scores, symphonic poems and such like, Lambert always stood out against the use of the more titanic composers, such as Beethoven, Brahms, or even Mozart, as being fatally unsuited to choreography. The correctness of this advice has certainly been confirmed by most of the choreographic experiments, which have seen the light of day. A typically shrewd and adventurous choice was the tone-poem *Paris* by Delius for the ballet *Nocturne*, certainly one of the most moving and musical of Ashton's creations. Later successful ballets were built on such foundations as Schubert's *Wanderer Fantasy*, Franck's *Symphonic Variations*, and Tchaikovsky's dynamic, but seldom played *Hamlet*.

Some of the greatest mainstays of the repertoire have been the scores collected and rearranged from piano-music or operas. *Les Patineurs* and *Les Rendezvous* were brilliantly extracted from Meyerbeer and Auber, and have proved ideal bases for *divertissements*. Purcell was delightfully pillaged and adapted for the ballet *Comus*, and even Bach was safe in the hands of Sir William Walton, whose beautiful score for *The Wise Virgins* has become so popular in the concert hall. Liszt, however, was really the chief of Lambert's 'lost' composers, and the long ballet *Apparitions*, for which he also composed the theme, affords a magnificent panorama of the work of this unsettled genius. His *Dante Sonata*, for solo piano, was also rearranged as a piano concerto.

This is not the place to discuss the musical merits of the new scores of this period. The important factor is that their success emerged from collaboration in the best tradition, between composer, choreographer, and musical director, and that the guiding hand was there to steer towards the best results. Gavin Gordon's *Rake's Progress*, Toye's *Haunted Ballroom*, Berners' *Wedding Bouquet*, Lambert's *Horoscope*, and Bliss' *Checkmate* are outstanding examples, which have stood the test of time. Vaughan Williams' magnificent *Job* had been written for the Camargo Society, and could now make its full impression with the increased musical resources.

The same musical policy has been continued at Covent Garden, as far as the intrusion of world tours will permit. During the last four seasons the twelve new ballets have comprised six original scores, four established scores (including the three-act *Sylvia*), and two adaptations, from the works of Chabrier and Donizetti. Six is certainly not a large total of new scores, but it must be remembered that the company's working conditions are vastly different from the pre-war days. At Sadler's Wells performances averaged one and a half per week during the resident season, and these were played before an audience of fanatical 'regulars', who could not only be depended on to come and come again, but

SOUTH WEST VIEW of
from a Drawing by

SADLER'S WELLS,
R. C. Andrews. 1792.

London, Published, 1 June 1814.

by Robert Wilkinson, N.º 58 Cornhill.

VIEW OF THE THEATRE IN ITS FORMER STATE.

View of the Sadler's Wells Theatre, 1792

to encourage all forms of new endeavour. At Covent Garden it is necessary to fill a large opera house for seven performances a week, during large portions of the year, and this is done by attracting a huge new public, interested and enthusiastic, but largely uninformed, who come to be entertained and charmed rather than to criticise the latest experiments. This public frankly prefers Tchaikovsky and Delibes, and it becomes a matter of careful timing to insert the new works, at moments when it is possible for the company to rehearse them adequately. Just as many works, which could be successfully staged at Sadler's Wells, would be overwhelmed by the chilling magnificence of Covent Garden, so the acoustic differences of the two theatres have their effect on the suitability of musical scores. At Sadler's Wells the sound of an orchestra of fifty players, or less, is bright, loud, and ebullient, and these qualities are of the greatest help to the dancers. All the climaxes of drama or ensemble are supported by an exciting noise from the pit, and even the thinnest orchestral texture is vividly conveyed to all parts of the house.

At Covent Garden a full symphony orchestra (75–80 players) produces about the right amount of accompaniment for grand opera, and the mellow sound from the sunken

View of the New Theatre Royal, Covent Garden, 1810

pit is not unduly loud for the singers. Only when the orchestra is inflated to about 100 players, for such works as *Electra, Wozzeck,* or *The Ring,* does the blaze of tone become really arresting. The lack of vividness and brilliance is a very real handicap to the ballet, who in any case cannot use more than about sixty players for most of the year. These musical resources are of course greatly superior to those available to most ballet companies, but when one considers the size of orchestra which is considered essential in continental opera houses, particularly Vienna and Milan, it is not to be expected that sixty players can present the heaviest Tchaikovsky ballet-scores as effectively as ninety or a hundred.

Composers of new works are nearly always disappointed at the dimness of the sound at Covent Garden, and this is not helped by their normal habit of standing with the choreographers at the back of the Grand Tier, the worst place in the house for sound, where reflection from the roof is cut off by the balcony above, and only percussion and tuba are clearly audible. The upper, cheaper parts of the house, and the extreme back of the stalls have much the best acoustics. American opera houses are much kinder to ballet performances, because the orchestral pits can be raised until the players are almost on a level with the audience, and the sound becomes a more integral part of the performance. Chicago, which has a seating capacity some two and a half times as large as Covent Garden, is particularly rewarding in this respect.

The choice of music for a new ballet and the fitting of movements to the music may come about in various ways. Choreographers are naturally addicted to listening to gramophone records, like hungry prospectors searching for untapped resources. If they are important enough to insist on following their own fancy, the results may be successful or disastrous, as too many examples have shown. A few choreographers have professional musical training, but the most consistently successful members of the tribe will almost certainly discuss the matter with friends in the musical profession, and the musical director, with whom they can then co-operate at the piano, in the fitting of the script into the frame of the music.

With newly commissioned scores, the practice of allowing the choreographer to choose the composer, with whom he may happen to feel the greatest affinity, can also bring success or failure. Looking back over the last forty years of ballet history, one can see that the most brilliant results have usually been gained by the individual suggestions of either the directors or the musical directors of the companies. At Covent Garden there is now an advisory board, where suggestions are pooled. This is a wise and necessary institution for any company, which can be made to carry the dreaded and unmerited stigma 'supported by the taxpayer'.

The closest co-operation between composer, choreographer, and musical director is most desirable, before any notes are written. Timings and tempi can be fully discussed, before they become sources of agitation and argument later in the proceedings. When commercial gramophone records are not available, it is a good idea to make a piano recording of the music, which the choreographer can then play to his heart's content in his own drawing-room. The musical director should be on hand during this period to clarify rhythmical complexities or explain the structure of the work. Some choreographers prefer to split up the musical phrases into set numbers of beats (always known as 'counts') and decide on the steps before they go near the rehearsal room. Others feel themselves restricted by these rigid bonds, and like to soak themselves in the music at home, so that at rehearsal their knowledge of the music and the actual physical presence of the dancers will suggest the movements, which are the most naturally musical and the most apt for the artists concerned. It is very important for the musical director to attend most of the initial rehearsals, so that the tempi can be established beyond doubt: but the real brunt of the early work is borne by the rehearsal pianists. Apart from their long hours of endless repetition, they inevitably find themselves in the position of general secretary to the choreographer. There is no established method of noting down ballet-steps for future reference, and marginal notes in the piano scores become the vital referenda for all rehearsals and revivals. Poor pianists—how often are they to be seen—after being scolded and shouted at for hours, calmly and kindly settling a dispute over the correct steps, between dancers and choreographer: and when the premiere of a new work arrives, their tremendous contribution to the performance receives no applause or bouquets. It is indeed fortunate for dancers, that there are these expert musicians, whose love for the ballet enables them to rise above the drudgery of their work.

The first dress rehearsal of a new ballet is normally carried through to piano accompaniment. This gives full scope for the inevitable wastage of time over dresses, lighting, etc.: meanwhile the conductor has two or sometimes three (for a long work) orchestral rehearsals, during the last of which the company is invited to run through the work with the orchestra, so that they can gain some preliminary knowledge of the orchestral texture. This is still a musical rehearsal, and should firmly be kept free from minor interruptions by the choreographer or stage-manager. At the final orchestral dress rehearsal the conductor must consider himself at the disposal of the stage, and he will be fortunate if time permits any but the most minor musical repairs.

The first question put to any ballet conductor is always, "Tell me, do you follow the dancers or do they follow you?" This is impossible to answer directly, as the repertoire of any major ballet company covers a large range of co-operation between stage and orchestra pit, from playing the music 'straight' and regardless of the stage, to the most exact timing of the end of pirouettes and lifts or the most comfortable speed of fouettées for a particular ballerina. In the long classical ballets, the conductor is naturally in command for mime scenes and character dances, and for most of the smaller variations the tempo should be set and inflexible. But the correct presentation of a grand pas de deux or a ballerina's variation calls for all sorts of understanding and tolerance, as they are full of the sort of movements, which are entirely subject to the techniques and physiques of particular dancers. It must however be emphasized that for all types of music, from the symphonies, concertos, and symphonic poems to the charming banalities of *Giselle*, an appreciation of the movements and of the dramatic content of the ballet should be controlling factors of all performances. Minute variations of tempo can help so much without harming the music, and the same tempo can sound too fast or too slow or just right according to the manner in which it is played and conducted. The correct rhythmical force and dramatic point can only be given by a conductor who views the ballet as a whole and not just another orchestral score. A sense of movement is a much surer guide than the marking of scores with metronome speeds, which can only be temporary aids.

It is of great assistance to a ballet conductor to be a fluent pianist. It is one thing to sit next to an experienced rehearsal pianist, listening to the tempi and beating time, and quite another matter to sit down and set the tempo oneself. It is fairly certain that, if one can play the score on the piano to the satisfaction of the dancers, one will be able to set the tempi in the pit with a good deal of confidence and certainty.

All new ballet conductors are sure to be asked to conduct difficult scores without rehearsal, and they will also be called upon before long to rehearse difficult works with mediocre orchestras in various languages, with about one third of the requisite rehearsal time. There are a number of stages in the maturity of the conductor. He will be regarded at first with moderately disguised alarm and suspicion by the dancers, but if he shows interest in the stage and ability to understand the movements, he will soon be accepted and welcomed. He will now be much gratified to be considered as the dancers' friend, and will take pride in helping their difficulties to an unlimited degree. Experience should bring the knowledge that indiscriminate surrender to the foibles of dancers is not only musically disastrous in the long run but extremely bad for the standards of the whole ballet company as well as the individuals concerned. Nerves and fatigue affect dancers in many different ways: some will genuinely benefit from a little extra time and latitude, but others will take the opportunity to dawdle and hesitate. The attack and sharpness of their performance will suffer, whereas an extra 'bite' and ruthlessness in the tempo will just give them the stimulus needed to strengthen and tighten up their work.

However we may try and insist that a dance is created to the correct tempo, it will always be possible for the dancers to go much faster when they are thoroughly familiar with the steps. One is often scolded at rehearsals for rushing dances at tempi which subsequently prove unduly leisurely: and a slippery stage or fatigue may cause even the most musical dancers to complain of being hurried at the exact tempi which have been agreed on at rehearsals. At the same time it is wise not to take the opinions of the dancers too literally: small variations of tempo can spoil the effect of a solo, but the most minute differences invariably receive such comments as "That was *terribly* slow, *terribly* fast," or "were you anxious to catch a train?"

These are some of the problems in the day-to-day life of the ballet conductor. Only the dancers really know how the conductor can make or mar a performance; and a sprightly performance by the conductor, which has created many difficulties for the dancers, will often receive much more favourable notices than a carefully integrated performance, where obvious sensational effects have sometimes to be eschewed in order to give time and point to the movements.

Ballet has now an enormous public, of which a large proportion are normally unmusical theatre-goers. This sometimes makes the conductor feel that he might as well start the gramophone record and read the paper during the performance. But there is no doubt that even the unmusical public appreciate (if unconsciously) the presence of a full-scale and adequate musical accompaniment: and it would probably be correct to say that ballet-music has discovered more people's musical sensibilities than any other form of music. As for the musical profession, the great popularity of ballet has led to the formation of so many balletic enterprises with inadequate musical resources, that most musicians tend to regard the ballet-conductor as one who is prepared to hack through the scores at grossly distorted tempi and with a skeleton of the original orchestration. That such enterprises are usually successful is an additional source of irritation. One of our leading music critics has described ballet as a minor art compared with opera. Was there ever such pretentious nonsense? To musicians and the musically informed, opera is naturally the most fascinating subject because it is the most highly developed and complex form of music-making. But dancing, and the watching of dancing, is one of the oldest, simplest, and most elemental activities of the human race.

Perhaps the most rewarding factor of the conductor's life is his acceptance into a world which has no parallel in the theatrical or musical profession, for its humanity and practicality. By reason of their highly specialized training from an early age, dancers are apt to form something of a 'closed shop' against outsiders, but once their friendship is given, it is not only loyal and warm, but sincere, and one looks over at the internecine warfare of the opera world with little regret. Whether these have always been the characteristics of ballet companies is perhaps open to doubt, from the stories that are told of Russian days: but from some years' experience of a great British company, it can be said with certainty that, wherever life may lead one in the future, one will not find a set of companions more delightful, amusing, or kind.

Music

Constant Lambert at the Conductor's desk

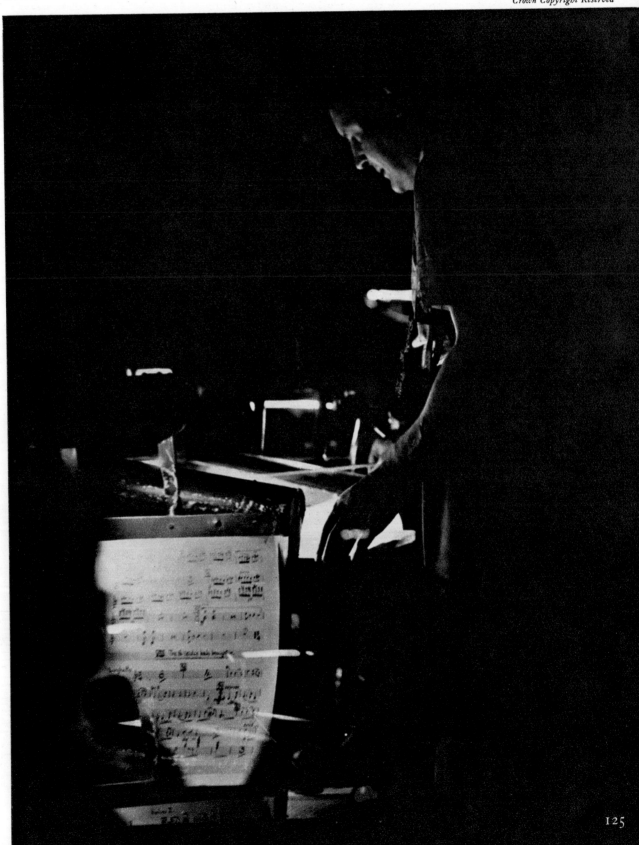

Baron

Constant Lambert at rehearsal

Edwin Evans

Lord Berners and Gertrude Stein

Frederick Ashton, Lord Berners and Constant Lambert

Dudley Styles

Vaughan Williams, O.M.

'*Job*'—*Elihu with the Three Comforters*

Edward Mandinia

Derek Allen

Sir Arthur Bliss

B.B.C.

Sir William Walton

129

Jean Gilbert, solo pianist

Angus McBean

John Hollingsworth, conductor

Maurice Seymour

130

At Rehearsal: Robert Irving conducts, Dame Ninette de Valois watches the stage

' *Le Spectre de la Rose* '

Rex Whistler's *drop curtain*

132

BALLET DÉCORS

Kenneth Clark

THE history of ballet décor in the last fifty years involves a conflict between flat and deep: between the stage conceived as a picture and the stage conceived as an extension of the auditorium. At first ballet existed only in depth. The dancers, mimes, or masqueraders came down a long hall, with groves or fountains arranged at the sides, and perhaps a temple at the end. When, towards the end of the 16th century, theatrical representation began to take place on what we should call a stage the illusion of great depth was maintained by false perspectives; and although the choreography of these early ballets is lost to us, we can infer that their movement was always three dimensional. The plan was as important as the elevation. For two centuries ballet was closely related to architecture, and like the processions and festivals which occupied so much of a renaissance artist's time, the impermanence of its settings had an uninhibiting effect, and permitted flights of fancy in which the architect could try out new inventions. Inigo Jones' Whitehall reproduces with little variation the approved Italian models, his designs for masquerade scenery are daringly inventive; and at the end of the 17th century Berain, one of the greatest of all ballet designers, may be said to have originated a new style of architecture, the Rococo. This convention of architectural scenery, in which the dancers move in a sumptuous, fantastic and apparently endless space, was maintained in the earliest ballets of Diaghilev, by both Benois and Bakst. Benois had an unrivalled gift for assimilating the styles of other times and places. His reform of the Petersburg stage was largely a return to earlier historical models. But even Bakst, who once seemed so deliciously modern, often drew his inspiration from Gissy or the Bibienas.

Fantasy and elaboration were the product of a royal or imperial opera house. But décor of this kind was expensive to produce and difficult to move; and perhaps it was inevitable that when Diaghilev's own company began to spend most of its time on tour a simpler and more pictorial style was evolved. Actually *Le Carnaval*, which had been improvised for a charity performance, seems to have been the first modern ballet to take place before the kind of simple setting which has since become commonplace necessity. The idea of dancing before a flat curtain was accelerated by Nijinski's choreography, for although *l'Après-midi d'un Faune* originally had an elaborately painted drop-scene by Bakst, the action, inspired by archaic Greek reliefs, is all on one plane, and an illusion of depth was positively harmful. These tendencies were accelerated by the 1914 war which cut off Diaghilev from the tradition of the old Imperial ballet, and at the same time familiarized him with that revolution in the arts which had been taking place in Paris during the very years that his ballet had been appearing there. Painting was abandoning the long attempt to imitate appearances, and was seeking to influence the mind directly through the eye by shapes and colours and unconscious associations. As a result shapes had become more accentuated and colours brighter; there was a more immediate impact on the senses; and this was exactly what Diaghilev required. The Russian Ballet and the post-Impressionist painters seem to have been waiting for one another. Actually the first effort to employ one of the masters of the movement, Picasso's *Parade*, was not a great success, simply because it was based on the architectural element in modern painting, analytical cubism, and not on the pictorial—what we now call *fauveism*—which contained the necessary element of liberated colour. But Diaghilev's next two commissions to distinguished painters—Derain's *Boutique Fantasque* and Picasso's *Tricorne* produced the most successful décors and costumes of our time. The choice showed great insight: also an element of luck. Derain was still a genial pasticheur, with a gift for decoration which was soon to be lost in the heavy, respectable exhibition pictures of the next decade. As for Picasso, his amazing adaptability and instinctive feeling for a new means of expression enabled him to invent for Diaghilev a style which has become a model for the best scene designers of the last thirty years.

The unqualified success of *Boutique* and *Tricorne* led to the belief that any distinguished painter of the modern movement could be employed on ballet design. But even under Diaghilev's guidance and with the *élan* of the post-impressionist movement unspent, this was proved to be an illusion. Some artists whose style seemed appropriate to stage design were concentrated on pictorial problems and unwilling to relate such problems to the needs of the theatre. It is well known that Henri Matisse resented the suggestions that his brightly-patterned paintings are decoration, and this was born out by the failure (in spite of *La Rossignol*) of his décors. Unfortunately I never saw *Les Fâcheux* of Braque or *L'Amour Vainqueur* of Juan Gris, so cannot judge of their success as décors, although I have no doubt about the pleasure they must have given the eye on the rise of the curtain. Others of the artists whom Diaghilev employed in his later and less purposeful period were obviously pure easel painters such as Utrillo or Beauchant, who could do no more than offer one of their pictures to be translated into a back drop. In these instances qualities necessary to theatrical presentation were lost; moreover, the habit of dancing in front of a drop curtain continued the flatness of Nijinski's choreography, and deprived the ballet of one of its chief beauties, the animation of architectural space. And yet these late experiments with painters had two things to recommend them: first, that it is exceedingly difficult to know in advance which painter is likely to be successful: Rouault, for example would have seemed less adaptable than Matisse, and entirely wrapped up in the pictorial realization of his private world; yet in the *Prodigal Son* he succeeded in translating the strange quality of his imagination into theatrical terms. And secondly, even if a distinguished artist fails to adapt his style to the theatre, he may contribute some new principle of shape and colour which the professional stage designer could not hope to discover for himself. Such discoveries are, after all, the result of contemplation and solitary struggle; and a life connected with the theatre is a life of action and hourly accommodation. So that even the most uncompromisingly 'private' artist may be of value to stage design as kind of shock-treatment for the lethargy of professionalism.

I have dwelt so long on the Diaghilev ballet because we can now look at it with some degree of historical detachment; and the problems of stage design which confronted it are still those of the Sadler's Wells ballet today. There is, however, an important difference. Diaghilev was working at an inspiring moment, when the prevailing style seemed capable of indefinite expansion. Such moments in the history of art do not last long—usually not more than twenty years; and the best designs of Derain and Picasso were done thirty-five years ago. Some of the painters are still alive, but the post-impressionist movement has long ago died. There is no single centre of art, and no new group of artists which excites us in the way we were excited by the *École de Paris* of the '20's. There is therefore less inducement to use non-theatrical painters and less of that compelling desire to be 'in the movement', which, for better or worse, drove Diaghilev to try every rising star in French art.

The Russian ballet started sumptuous, static and traditional, and ended simple, portable and revolutionary. Sadler's Wells has followed the opposite course. The early ballets had to be exceedingly economical and the décors were correspondingly simple. To make simplicity effective requires professional skill, and some of the most successful of Sadler's Wells' creations were the work of stage designers William Chappell and Sophie Fedorovitch. The latter had a genius for simplification. A curtain, a cloud, a few lines were all that she required to create an atmosphere in harmony with the music and the choreographer's invention. What may be called the early Sadler's Wells' style, the style of some of Ashton's finest ballets, is due partly to the austere and subtle influence of Sophie Fedorovitch.

In these early productions Sadler's Wells also employed easel painters with happy results. Both John Armstrong's productions of *Façade*, for example, were perfectly adapted to the scale and weight of a ballet which was serious only in its perfect art. They were the not unworthy grandchildren of *Boutique*. Helpmann's *Miracle of the Gorbals* on the other hand was a horrifying, message-bearing work very far from the spirit of Diaghilev, and Edward Burra's décor is remote from the fantasies of the *École de Paris*. Yet because Burra is a fine painter it escapes that cinematographic expressionism which has afflicted many ballets of the same kind on the Continent. The sinister atmosphere of the shipyards was created largely by the admirable drop curtain lowered during the introductory music. When still at the Wells the ballet also employed two English painters who have since become famous, Graham Sutherland and John Piper. Sutherland's décor for Ashton's *Wanderer*, although no more than two back drops, was of a high imaginative beauty, and one cannot but regret that he has not been commissioned by the ballet again, for if he had been given the chance to grow familiar with the technique of stage design, he might have extended the boundaries

Rex Whistler's sketch for the drop curtain for ' The Rake's Progress '

of that intense, visionary world which is concentrated in his paintings. Piper, of course, continued to work for the stage, mastered its technicalities, and has done a number of décors of great distinction. His sense of the character of his medium has allowed him to achieve richness without littleness; yet to my mind one of his most successful designs was one of the simplest, the setting of Cranko's *Sea Change*, where a few necessary symbols, given their full decorative value, told the story, delighted the eye and remained a background to the dancing.

Two of the early successes of Sadler's Wells which must also be mentioned are *Checkmate* and *The Rake's Progress*. Both were the work of Ninette de Valois, but from the point of view of décor they were a complete contrast. *Checkmate*, by MacKnight Kaufer, was a brilliant synthesis of modern 'isms—Cubism, Futurism, and the Syncretism of Kandinsky, all made more immediate for impact in the theatre. For this reason it has been one of the most popular of English ballets on the Continent but has remained slightly outside the spirit of Sadler's Wells. On the other hand *The Rake's Progress* by Rex Whistler is sober and factual and we are hardly conscious of the décor and costumes until we realize how much they contribute to the success of the ballet as a whole. Rex Whistler had an unsurpassed memory for the details of ornament and costume, which he could reproduce and recombine with astonishing fluency. He also had a considerable architectural sense and his death in the war was a real disaster for English stage design, for, with the greater opportunities of Covent Garden, his talent would certainly have expanded, and we should have seen some of the most splendid settings in depth since the *Pavillon d'Armide* of Benois.

When the Sadler's Wells ballet moved to Covent Garden the austere economies of its earlier days were no longer essential. Sophie Fedorovitch maintained her characteristic simplicity, and even gave it a new quality by using it on a larger scale. But on the whole the tendency was towards elaboration. The opening performance was a production of *Sleeping Beauty* by Oliver Messel as fanciful and extravagant as that of Bakst in 1921. It lacked, no doubt, Bakst's bizarre inventiveness and underlying sense of draughtsmanship; but it was more digestible and perhaps more suited to the spirit of Perrault. Messel had already provided for Sadler's Wells Theatre a charming setting of *Comus*; and in the same year (1943) there had been discovered another master of elaboration, Leslie Hurry, whose décor for Helpmann's *Hamlet* revealed a highly original and slightly disturbing talent. Hurry was entrusted with the other masterpiece of Petipa, *Swan Lake*, with remarkable results. In contrast with Messel's amiable acceptance of all the material which the past has to offer, Hurry gives every detail the stamp of his own strange imagination. His fertility of invention is most impressive, but perhaps, since *Hamlet*, he has not had a commission which allows full scope for his gift of macabre hallucination. The third full-length ballet at Covent Garden, Ashton's beautiful re-arrangement of *Sylvia*, was also given to a painter with a passion for elaborate detail, Robin Ironside. His designs are poetical, and in harmony with the music of Delibes, but inevitably the décors of these three ambitious productions have lacked some of the freshness and adventurous brightness of the earlier ballets at Sadler's Wells theatre.

I have said that Picasso's *Tricorne* provided a model for ballet design up to the present day. The reason is that it showed how space can be suggested by purely pictorial means. The formal architectural settings of the eighteenth century no longer correspond with the speed of our impressions and the freedom of our associations. The modern setting in depth requires a breadth of treatment in keeping with the broad effects and massed movements of the dancers. Designers must achieve their ends by suggestion rather than by detailed statement, and must recognize that the stage picture is an illusion, intended to carry a certain distance, and not a fact to be inspected in detail. The scenery should be subordinate to the dancers, and for this reason the costumes have, since *Tricorne*, become stronger and more emphatic than the background. In devising the sets economy of means is a positive merit, because it stimulates the imagination; and proliferation of detail is positively wearisome, because every time the imagination tries to escape on its own it finds the road blocked. The French designers have never forgotten this, and of all who learned the lessons of *Tricorne* and *Boutique*, the most brilliant and enchanting was Christian Bérard. He had in the highest degree a sense of the theatrically effective, and the simplicity with which he achieved these effects had a quality of wit, of impudence, almost, which was irresistible. But this was made possible by a mastery of pictorial expression, of drawing and colour in their strict art-school application, which made his slightest indications convincing. For this reason alone no English designer has approached his skill, and, for that matter, he has had no successor in France. But it remains true that one of the most delightful sets commissioned by the Sadler's Wells ballet since it came to Covent Garden is the work of a designer from Paris, *Balabile* by Clavé, where space is no longer emphasized by a colonnade in perspective, but is suggested by a curtain, a railing or a few ropes artfully lit and disposed. It may be contrasted with Osbert Lancaster's *Bonne Bouche*, which, witty and appropriate though it is, is no more than the enlargement of one of Lancaster's incomparable caricatures of architecture. Clavé's settings, although they have the colour and character of his paintings, are entirely theatrical, and delight us by ingenious (and in fact misleading) economy of effect. They are the work of a transforming imagination.

Covent Garden has shown courage in continuing to employ non-theatrical artists in spite of disappointments; the size of the stage makes experiments expensive and the management must often have been tempted to fall back on designers of proved professional skill, like James Bailey or Vlakevitch. In consequence we may expect more experimental work in the Sadler's Wells theatre ballet. But perhaps what is needed now is not so much more enterprise as a steadier and more attentive employment of those artists who have already proved a talent for stage design. For a young painter to make his first attempt on the enormous stage of Covent Garden is a daunting experience—no one would dream of using a singer or dancer in that way; and yet there are several who have been employed once with success, John Craxton's *Daphnis and Chloe* is an example, and have not been employed again. This is bad policy; for the designer must not only master the technical resources of the theatre: he must be on friendly terms with the choreographer, the leading dancers, the wardrobe mistress, the scene painters, the electricians and all those who contribute to the complex art of the theatre. And this sense of intimacy must not only be technical, but must involve an interchange of ideas and a common purpose. Such was the character of Diaghilev's 'committee', both in its early stages, and afterwards with Stravinsky, Cocteau, and Picasso in Rome; and such, on a more modest scale, was originally the character of the Ballet at Sadler's Wells. Critics and rivals are quick to complain of a coterie, but in fact every creative movement is the result of a coterie which becomes grand, respectable and inevitable when seen in the evening light of history. If the ballet décors at Covent Garden are to fulfil the promise of Sadler's Wells what is wanted is not more money, but community of feeling, stimulating discussion, and ample time for preparation.

Sets and Costumes

Costume design for 'The Rake's Progress,' by Rex Whistler

Hogarth's 'The Rake's Progress'

Tun
Ltd.

Tun
Ltd.

J. W. Debenham

'The Rake's Progress'

Rex Whistler's sets and costumes

Rex Whistler

Set for 'The Wise and Foolish Virgins' by Rex Whistler

J. W. Debenham

Lord Berners' set and costumes for 'Wedding Bouquet'

*Cecil Beaton, design, set and costumes
for the Ballroom scene of 'Apparitions'*

Coppelia

Osbert Lancaster's design for Act I. Covent Garden, 1954

John Armstrong's set and costumes for 'Façade'

John Piper's first designs for ballet : ' The Quest '

*(opposite) Graham Sutherland's set.
and costumes for ' The Wanderer '*

Sets and costumes by Edward Burra

(opposite top) ' *Miracle in the Gorbals* '
(bottom) ' *Barabau* '

Edward Burra : Drop curtain for ' Don Quixote '

Leslie Hurry

(opposite) ' *Lac des Cygnes* '

' *Lac des Cygnes* ' : *The Ballroom*

(opposite) Oliver Messel 'Homage à la Rein

Sophie Fedorovitch

Costumes and décor
for 'Dante Sonata'
inspired by Flaxman

Felix Fonteyn

153

Felix Fontey

'*Sylvia*': *Act I.   Décor and Costumes by Robin and Christopher Ironside*

(*opposite*) *Osbert Lancaster's* '*Coppelia*'

(*overleaf*)

(*left*) *Osbert Lancaster's* '*Pineapple Poll*'

(*right*) *Osbert Lancaster's* '*Bonne Bouche*'

SOME PROBLEMS
OF BALLET TODAY

Ninette de Valois

I AM often asked what, in my opinion, is the most significant aspect of our ballet today, and my answer is the acceptance of this art as a vital part of our contemporary theatre. This recognition does not end with our position as a separate branch of cultural entertainment, for it brings in its wake a further influence, namely, the effect of the ballet on the production of much of the contemporary opera and classical drama.

We know that the classical ballet was born 300 years ago with the contemporary modern theatre, and played its part alongside the opera and drama until a short period of inglorious decline towards the end of the last century reduced the importance of its position. Until then, as it now succeeds in doing again, it infused into the theatre in general those aspects of the dance that form an integral part of many theatrical presentations. Mime, period movement, poise and carriage are the gifts of the ballet to actor and singer, and the understanding of mass movement and of grouping is our contribution to the technique of the producer. Indeed, the work of the early ballet masters of the French Court stretched far beyond their groups of professional dancers. The correspondence between David Garrick and Noverre makes fascinating reading, for it shows the great actor in a generous mood, bestowing his patronage on the famous ballet master, and expressing his undoubted belief in the influence of Noverre on the theatre.

But it must be admitted that there was a moment during the last decade in England when the influence of the ballet on the production of classical drama became somewhat exaggerated. I have frequently stated how depressing it is to see a 'bad ballet' instead of a good dramatic production, and Sir John Gielgud raised his voice some months ago in a firmly expressed opinion on the present-day tendency of 'balletic' production of classical plays. But this phase is now under control and our influence, consequently, has a more dignified part to play.

The rise of the classical ballet of late, and the demand for full-length classical works, show a healthy reaction on the part of both the general and the specialized audience. Herein lie our beginnings, and our future tradition will evolve from such contacts none the worse for such exacting task-masters. Sadler's Wells, the largest subsidized ballet in England, is not yet a quarter of a century old. Consider the importance of its tie with this classical tradition, and the effect on the mental discipline and visual discrimination of today's young audience and artist, and realize its influence on the choreographer of tomorrow.

I must now try to answer a question that is asked with unfailing regularity—"What do I feel about modern ballet?" "What is its position in relation to the classical?" "Is it a challenge?" Firstly, I bother myself little about my feelings or those of my contemporaries. Secondly, its 'position in relation to' is a journalistic cliché, endeavouring economically and æsthetically to answer a question that is neither definable nor founded on common reasoning. Thirdly, creative work is not necessarily an aggressive 'challenge'. It should be a virile natural force introducing new forms in each succeeding generation.

Today, as yesterday, in all fields of creative work we are expressing our contemporary thoughts, ideals and beliefs. This is all in order and all to the good, and let us not be puzzled or pained when we realize that we cannot see the wood for the trees. The choreographer, dramatist or musician of any country is either self-consciously of his age or a 'time-traveller'. But all forms of creative work of any epoch are dominated by their artists' sense of destruction or construction; in other words, we express through channels of revolution or evolution, and in many cases—in particular in that type of work coyly labelled 'provocative'—we are too close to our own times to judge what is on the ascent or descent with any true clarity of thought.

It is only a man of unusual vision who can discern with unfailing surety between these two fundamentals in relation to all creative work happening in his time. The average man is rooted within the midst of the ensuing turmoil. Was it not the same one hundred years ago? How few of the ballets of the great Petipa have survived the passage of time? But it matters little; for the part speaks for the whole, and we are now content to see only the best ballets of the great masters of the past as a means of obtaining a sense of proportion towards their particular period. The same may be said for the first twenty-five years of the modern classical ballet. The surviving repertoire of the Diaghilev era is a modest one, taking into account the fact that the Company was in existence for twenty years.

All modern tendencies in the ballets of Europe and America are today in a hesitant mood, and they, of course, consist of good, bad and indifferent works. That we may frequently misjudge or misunderstand each other is a good sign; it may well mean that we are unconsciously showing certain national characteristics, without which the art of a country becomes devitalized.

But for a moment I would speak personally of today's short contemporary ballet, and I would speak of it in general. It is packed with involved movement and tortured symbolism, and I do not think that we need wait any longer to realize that the second half of this century should deal with something more than our present 'Ballet Digest'. We are in danger of choking ourselves with this condensed technical approach. Themes beg for development, movement needs more light and shade, more bridging should be permitted from one dance movement to another, and a sharp dividing line accepted and adhered to between mere acrobatics and the portrayal of lineal elegance.

The ballet's new architectural form could now be given a more gracious expansion, for the theatre is tired of the brief comment, and it awaits a leisurely, well-constructed statement. I suggest that the journalistic stage of modern ballet has had its day; it is time for the flowering of its true literature. So let us suppose that we have reached an important crossroad, where we will pause to recognize certain broad principles. The technique of today needs discipline and pruning, if it is to fulfil the demand now prevailing for full-length modern works. This must become, in our future plans, the joint responsibility of librettist, composer and choreographer. Modern artists of the dance have stated their case to the world for nearly half a century in short, sharp sentences; let them now endeavour to show us that their brief comments can end in a philosophy that is constructive, let them show that they recognize construction as of more importance than that half-way house to destruction—provocation for the sake of being provocative.

But it is firstly the problem of music, for sound can evoke a mood and stress a statement, with more speed and impact than visual movement. Music 'adapted' to ballet is an increasing menace; a return to the specially composed score is of primary importance, for here lies the true collaboration. When the choreographer, librettist and composer work together from the first on a new ballet composition they establish, at the outset, the intention to unify. It is that rarity, complete unity, that is both the simple and the complex answer to a successful work; failure is often and again not a matter of the 'choreography' or of the 'music' but an original oversight as to the relative values concerning the part with the whole. In the same way this 'unity' should underline the policy of a Company and the principles of its training school.

Our next effort lies in theatrical presentation, for once again choreography must accept the discipline and demands of the theatre. It must come to terms with the painter and his position in the theatre. We live in constant danger of losing all contact with those high standards set by Diaghilev concerning the perfect collaboration of choreography with décor and costume. In many countries Companies show equality of Terpsichorean material, but when it comes to the other Muses concerned, there are many and varied states of chaos.

Both in Europe and America the world is well served with established choreographers and promising members of the younger school. Dancers are numerous, and they are gifted, varied and exceedingly versatile. What we need is a spring-clean in the form of a general survey; we might tolerate a slogan. Dare I suggest 'Production Where Art Thou?'

Homage to the Queen

Costume designs by Oliver Messel, 1953

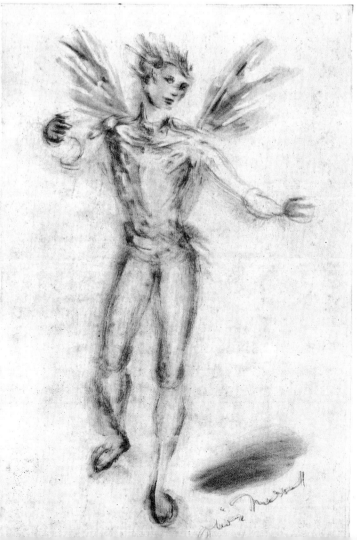

Masks and Faces

Jitendra Arya

Ninette de Valois

Rehearsal—Ninette de Valois and (seated on the floor) Violetta Elvin
(opposite) Alicia Markova as Giselle

In ' Les Sirènes '

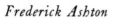

Frederick Ashton

In ' Nocturne '

As Doctor Coppelius

Frederick Ashton, Ninette de Valois and Leonide Massine

Angus McBean

Margot Fonteyn

Cecil Beaton

In ' Les Sirènes '

(opposite) In 'Apparitions '

Cecil Beaton

Margot Fonteyn in 'Tiresias'

(opposite) Margot Fonteyn in 'Sylvia'

Margot Fonteyn in 'The Sleeping Beauty' with Robert Helpmann

Margot Fonteyn in ' The Sleeping Beauty '

Robert Helpmann as Mr. O'Reilly in 'The Prospect Before Us'

Robert Helpmann as Satan in ' Job '

(opposite) Robert Helpmann in (top left) ' Miracle in the Gorbals ' (right)
' Comus ' (bottom left) ' The Sleeping Beauty ' (right) ' Wedding Bouquet '

George Balanchine   *Melton-Pippin*

Roland Petit   Ba[r]

Leonide Massine   *Baron*

Derek Allen

Andrée Howard

Alfred Rodrigues

Paul Tanqueray

Sol Hurok congratulates Margot Fonteyn

Felix Fonteyn

Ninette de Valois, Sol Hurok, Margot Fonteyn, George Balanchine, Beryl Grey after the première of 'Ballet Imperial'

Roger Wood

179

Moira Shearer as Odile in ' Swan Lake '

Moira Shearer as 'Cinderella'

Baron

Pamela May in ' Dante Sonata '

Baron

Violetta Elvin and John Field in 'Swan Lake'

Baron

Beryl Grey

Rowena Jackson and Michael Somes

Baron

Michael Somes

Michael Somes in ' Sylvia '

Alexis Rassine as The Blue Bird

John Field in ' Swan Lake '

John Hart

Baron

Denis de Marney

Brian Shaw in ' Les Patineurs '

Pauline Clayden in
'Daphnis and Chloe'

Roger Wood

Elaine Fifield in 'Reflection'

Julia Farron in ' Daphnis and Chloe '

Denis de Marney

Rosemary Lindsay in ' The Shadow '

Anne Heaton as Giselle

Philip Chatfield in 'Sylvia'

David Blair as Franz in 'Coppelia'

Appendix

A RECORD OF FIRST PRODUCTIONS, REVIVALS, AND
THEIR CASTS FROM THE FOUNDATION OF THE
SADLER'S WELLS BALLET UNTIL THE PRESENT DAY

*Although every effort has been made to ensure
accuracy and completeness, there are bound to be
both errors and omissions in the lists. For these
the editors apologise, and would be most grateful
to anyone who can point them out*

The Sadler's Wells Ballet—Vic-Wells

1931-1944

1941-45. *Their first three short seasons at the New Theatre, London, in 1941 were presented by Edward Wyndham and Bronson Albery. From October 1942 to June 1944 Bronson Albery acted as Administrator of the Ballet both in and out of London. It was during this period that the Company's name first became The Sadler's Wells Ballet*

SUITE DE DANSE

Music by Bach, arranged by Goossens
Scenery and costumes by Owen P. Smyth
Choreography by Ninette de Valois

First performance at Sadler's Wells Theatre 15th May, 1931
(Old Vic performance 18th December 1930)

CAST

Ninette de Valois, Joy Newton, Beatrice Appleyard, Sheila McCarthy, Freda Bamford, Ursula Moreton, Anita Hill, Barbara Jeffs, Alyce Meagher, Joan Day, Nadina Newhouse, Anton Dolin, Stanley Judson

HOMMAGE AUX BELLES VIENNOISES

Music by Schubert, arranged by Norman Franklin
Scenery and costumes by Owen P. Smyth
Choreography by Ninette de Valois

First performed at Sadler's Wells Theatre 15th May, 1931
(First produced at Old Vic 19th December, 1929)

CAST

Tyrolese	*Sheila McCarthy, Freda Bamford, Ivor Beddoes*
Pas de quatre	*Beatrice Appleyard, Nadina Newhouse Wendy Toye, Joan Day*
Pas de deux	*Joy Newton, Stanley Judson*
Pas de huit	*Monica Ratcliffe, Molly Ford, Marley Bell, Ida McIntyre, Marjorie Stewart, Phyllis Worthington, Mireille Bezaneon, Anita Hill*

THE FAUN

Music by Vaughan Williams
Costumes by Hedley Briggs
Choreography by Ninette de Valois

First performed at Sadler's Wells Theatre 15th May, 1931
(First Old Vic performance April, 1928)

CAST

Faun	*Stanley Judson*
Nymph	*Ursula Moreton*
Dryads	*Wendy Toye, Monica Ratcliffe, Marley Bell, Mollie Brown*

DANSES SACREES ET PROFANES

Music by Debussy
Costumes and masks by Hedley Briggs
Choreography by Ninette de Valois

First performed at Old Vic Theatre 5th May, 1931

CAST

Sacree	*Ursula Moreton Beatrice Appleyard, Joan Day, Phyllis Worthington, Marjorie Stewart*
Profane	*Freda Bamford, Joy Newton, Sheila McCarthy, Nadina Newhouse, Marley Bell*

LES PETITS RIENS

Music by Mozart
Scenery and costumes by Owen P. Smyth
Choreography by Ninette de Valois

First performance at Sadler's Wells Theatre 15th May,
1931
(First performance Old Vic 13th December, 1928)

CAST

ROSALIND	*Ninette de Valois*
CLYMENE	*Sheila McCarthy*
CORYDON	*Stanley Judson*
TRICIS	*Ivor Beddoes*
CORPS DE BALLET	*Monica Ratcliffe, Wendy Toye,*
	Ida McIntyre, Anita Hill,
	Barbara Jeffs, Alyce Meagher
CUPIDS	*Joy Robson, Mollie Brown*

❧

THE JACKDAW AND THE PIGEONS

Music by Hugh Bradford
Scenery and costumes by William Chappell
Choreography by Ninette de Valois

First performed at Sadler's Wells Theatre 15th May,
1931
(First performance Old Vic 5th May, 1931)

CAST

JACKDAW	*Ninette de Valois*
ATTENDANTS	*Beatrice Appleyard, Joan Day,*
	Joy Newton
PIGEONS	*Sheila McCarthy, Freda Bamford*
	Nadina Newhouse, Doreen Adams,
	Wendy Toye

❧

CEPHALUS AND PROCRIS

Music by Gretry
Scenery and costumes by William Chappell
Choreography by Ninette de Valois

First performed at the Sadler's Wells Theatre, 21st May,
1931
(First produced for Camargo Society 25th January, 1931)

CAST

CEPHALUS	*Stanley Judson*
PROCRIS	*Lydia Lopokova*
AURORA	*Ninette de Valois*
ATTENDANTS ON AURORA	*Beatrice Appleyard,*
	Joy Newton, Joan Day, Wendy Toye
ATTENDANTS ON CEPHALUS	*David Latoff, Robert Stuart,*
	Ivor Beddoes, Travis Kemp
DIANA'S FOLLOWERS	*Sheila McCarthy, Freda Bamford,*
	Doreen Adams, Nadina Newhouse

JOB

A Masque for Dancing in Eight Scenes

Book by Geoffrey Keynes
Music by Vaughan Williams
Scenery and costumes by Gwendolen Raverat
Choreography by Ninette de Valois

First revived at the Old Vic Theatre 22nd September,
1931

CAST

JOB	*John MacNair*
HIS WIFE	*Marjorie Stewart*
HIS THREE DAUGHTERS	*Ursula Moreton,*
	Marie Neilson, Doreen Adams
HIS SEVEN SONS	*Stanley Judson, Hedley Briggs,*
	Walter Gore, William Chappell,
	Claude Newman, Robert Stuart,
	Travis Kemp
THE THREE MESSENGERS	*Robert Stuart, Claude Newman*
	Travis Kemp
THE THREE COMFORTERS	*William Chappell,*
	Walter Gore, Hedley Briggs
WAR, PESTILENCE, FAMINE	*William Chappell,*
	Walter Gore, Hedley Briggs
ELIHU	*Stanley Judson*
SATAN	*Anton Dolin*
JOB'S SPIRITUAL SELF	*Gilding Clarke*

❧

REGATTA

Music by Gavin Gordon
Scenery and costumes by William Chappell
Choreography by Frederick Ashton

First performed at Sadler's Wells Theatre 7th October,
1931
(First performance Old Vic 22nd September, 1931)

CAST

CABIN BOY	*Stanley Judson*
THREE YACHTING GIRLS	*Freda Bamford,*
	Sheila McCarthy, Joy Newton
TWO YOUNG MEN	*Walter Gore, William Chappell*
	(Frederick Ashton 22.9.31)
FOREIGN VISITOR	*Ninette de Valois*

FÊTE POLONAISE

Music by Glinka
Costumes and scenery Owen P. Smyth
Choreography by Ninette de Valois
The figures of the Mazurka arranged by Stanley Judson

First performed at Sadler's Wells Theatre 23rd November,
1931

CAST

Phyllis Bedells and Stanley Judson in 1st 3 perfs.
Anthony Tudor and Keith Lester (11.1.32)
Alicia Markova (11.3.32)
Beatrice Appleyard, Joy Newton, Nadina Newhouse,
Monica Ratcliffe, Claude Newman, Mark Fawdry,
Travis Kemp

❦

JEW IN THE BUSH

Music by Gordon Jacob
Scenery and costumes by Bertram Guest
Choreography by Ninette de Valois

First performance at Old Vic Theatre 16th December,
1931

CAST

YOUTH	*Stanley Judson*
WITCH	*Freda Bamford*
BIRD	*Marie Nielson*
JEW	*Frederick Ashton*
QUEEN	*Ursula Moreton*
KING	*Travis Kemp*
EXECUTIONER	*Toni Repetto*
LORD CHAMBERLAIN	*John Greenwood*
HERALDS	*Monica Ratcliffe, Peggy Mellis*
	Molly Brown, Joy Robson
COURT LADIES	*Sheila McCarthy, Joy Newton,*
	Beatrice Appleyard, Nadina Newhouse,
	Gwyneth Matthews, Marley Bell

❦

NARCISSUS AND ECHO

Music by Arthur Bliss
Scenery and costumes by William Chappell
Choreography by Ninette de Valois

First performance at Sadler's Wells Theatre 30th January,
1932

CAST

ECHO	*Alicia Markova*
NARCISSUS	*Stanley Judson*
NYMPHS	*Ursula Moreton, Marie Nielson*
TWO SINGERS	*Alyce Nayler, Emlyn Bebb*

ROUT

Music by Arthur Bliss
Choreography by Ninette de Valois

First performance at Sadler's Wells Theatre 30th January,
1932

CAST

Ninette de Valois, Ursula Moreton, Joy Newton,
Beatrice Appleyard, Sheila McCarthy, Freda Bamford,
Nadina Newhouse, Marie Nielson, Travis Kemp,
Edward Garllard, Toni Repetto, Edward Hassall

SINGER

Alyce Naylor

❦

LE SPECTRE DE LA ROSE

Music by Weber
Choreography by Michel Fokine

First performed at the Old Vic Theatre, 4th March
1932

CAST

Ninette de Valois   *Anton Dolin*

❦

ITALIAN SUITE

Music by Lalo
Scenery and costumes by Phyllis Dolton
Choreography by Ninette de Valois

First performance at the Old Vic Theatre, 4th March,
1932

CAST

PRELUDE	*Ninette de Valois, Marie Nielson,*
	Ailne Phillips, Stanley Judson, Travis Kemp,
	Sheila McCarthy, Freda Bamford,
	Beatrice Appleyard, Joy Newton, Nadina Newhouse,
	Gwyneth Matthews
SERENADE	*Anton Dolin (also choreography)*
PAS DE DEUX (*music by Cottrau*)	*Ninette de Valois,*
	Anton Dolin

THE ENCHANTED GROVE

Music by Ravel and Debussy
Scenery and costumes by Duncan Grant
Choreography by Rupert Doone

First performed at Sadler's Wells Theatre 11th March, 1932

CAST

Eros	*Anton Dolin*
Psyche	*Alica Markova*
Courtesan	*Ninette de Valois*
Courier	*Rupert Doone*
Attendants	*Ursula Moreton, Marie Nielson*
Warriors	*Stanley Judson, Anthony Tudor*

❧

NURSERY SUITE

Music by Edward Elgar
Scenery and costumes by Nancy Allen
Choreography by Ninette de Valois

First performance at Sadler's Wells Theatre 19th March, 1932

CAST

Bo Peep	*Sheila McCarthy*
Georgy Porgy	*Anton Dolin*
Girls	*Ailne Phillips, Nadina Newhouse*
	Joan Day, Gwyneth Matthews,
	Peggy Mellis, Phyllis Worthington
Snow White	*Joy Newton*
Rose Red	*Beatrice Appleyard*
Three Bears	*Kurt Lenz, Travis Kemp,*
	Monica Ratcliffe
Jack	*Stanley Judson*
Jill	*Freda Bamford*
Prince and Princess	*Anton Dolin and Alicia Markova*

❧

DOUANES

Music by Geoffrey Toye (who conducted 1st perf.)
Scenery and costumes by Hedley Briggs
Choreography by Ninette de Valois

First performance at Sadler's Wells Theatre 11th October, 1932

CAST

Cook's Man	*Anton Dolin*
Passport Officer	*Anthony Tudor*
Tight Rope Dancer	*Ninette de Valois*
Husband	*John Greenwood*

Gendarmes	*Claude Newman, Travis Kemp,*
	Guy Massey
Eccentric Passenger	*Stanley Judson*
Young Ladies	*Marie Nielson, Beatrice Appleyard,*
	Monica Ratcliffe
Elderly Spinsters	*Joy Newton, Nadina Newhouse,*
	Gwyneth Matthews
Governess	*Ursula Moreton*
Little Girls	*Sheila McCarthy, Freda Bamford*
Little Boys	*Joy Robson, Molly Brown*

❧

THE LORD OF BURLEIGH

Scenario by Edwin Evans
Music by Mendelssohn, arranged by Edwin Evans,
orchestrated by Gordon Jacob
Scenery and costumes by George Shermshaw
Choreography by Frederick Ashton

First performed at the Old Vic Theatre 17th October, 1932

(First Camargo Society performance 15th December, 1931)

CAST

Katie Willows	*Alicia Markova*
Lady Clara Vere de Vere	*Ursula Moreton*
Lilian	*Sheila McCarthy*
Mariana	*Beatrice Appleyard*
Adeline	*Marie Nielson*
Madeline	*Nadina Newhouse*
Rosalind	*Ailne Phillips*
Margaret	*Freda Bamford*
Isabel	*Joy Newton*
Eleanor	*Gwyneth Matthews*
Lord of Burleigh	*Anton Dolin*
Edward Gray	*Travis Kemp*
Edwin Morris	*Anthony Tudor*
Eustace	*Claude Newman*

❧

THE ORIGIN OF DESIGN

Music by Handel, arranged by Sir Thomas Beecham
Scenery and costumes by William Chappell
Choreography by Ninette de Valois

First performed at Sadler's Wells Theatre 1st November, 1932

(First Camargo Society production 11th June, 1932)

CAST

Dibutade	*Ninette de Valois*
Her friends	*Nadina Newhouse, Joy Robson,*
	Elizabeth Miller

Eros	*Stanley Judson*
Attendants	*Claude Newman, Travis Kemp,*
	Guy Massey
Polydore	*Anton Dolin*
Apollo	*Anthony Tudor*
Muses	*Alicia Markova, Ursula Moreton,*
	Marie Nielson, Beatrice Appleyard,
	Freda Bamford, Joy Newton,
	Gwyneth Matthews, Joan Day,
	Ailne Phillips

☙

THE SCORPIONS OF YSIT

Music by Gavin Gordon
Scenery and costumes by Sophie Fedorovitch
Choreography by Ninette de Valois

First performance at the Sadler's Wells Theatre
15th November, 1932

CAST

Ysit	*Beatrice Appleyard*
Scorpions	*Freda Bamford, Sheila McCarthy,*
	Nadina Newhouse, Molly Brown,
	Joy Newton, Joan Day, Peggy Mellis
Marsh Women	*Ursula Moreton, Phyllis Worthington*

☙

BOLERO

Music by Ravel
Choreography by Anton Dolin

First performance at Sadler's Wells Theatre 6th December,
1932

SOLO BY
Anton Dolin

☙

PRIDE

Music by Scriabin, orchestrated by Gordon Jacob
Scenery and costumes by William Chappell
Choreography by Ninette de Valois

First performance at Sadler's Wells Theatre 3rd January,
1933

SOLO BY
Ninette de Valois

POMONA

Music by Constant Lambert
Scenery and costumes by Vanessa Bell
Choreography by Frederick Ashton

First performed at Sadler's Wells Theatre on
17th January, 1933
(First Camargo Society performance October. 1930)

CAST

Pomona	*Beatrice Appleyard*
Vertumnus	*Anton Dolin*
Attendants	*Freda Bamford, Ailne Phillips,*
	Joy Newton, Nadina Newhouse,
	Gwyneth Matthews, Joan Day,
	Hermione Darnborough, Peggy Mellis
Men	*Claude Newman, Travis Kemp*

☙

THE BIRTHDAY OF OBERON

Music by Purcell—" Faery Queen "
arranged by Constant Lambert
Scenery and costumes by John Armstrong
Choreography by Ninette de Valois

First performance at Sadler's Wells Theatre 7th February,
1933

CAST

Rural Dances

	Ailne Phillips, Joy Newton,
	Nadina Newhouse, Elizabeth Miller,
	Gwyneth Matthews, Claude Newman,
	Travis Kemp, Anthony Tudor, Guy Massey,
	Toni Repetto
2.	*Joy Robson, Mollie Brown, Jill Gregory*
3.	*Sheila McCarthy, Stanley Judson*
4.	*Ailne Phillips, Joy Newton,*
	Sheila McCarthy, Claude Newman, Travis Kemp
5.	*Ailne Phillips, Joy Newton,*
	Sheila McCarthy, Elizabeth Miller,
	Nadina Newhouse, Anita Hill,
	Gwyneth Matthews, Wenda Horsburgh, Joan Day,
	Daphne Tietgen, Di Brockwell,
	Phyllis Worthington, Stanley Judson,
	Claude Newman, Anthony Tudor, Guy Massey,
	Toni Repetto, Travis Kemp

Dance of the Seasons

Spring	*Beatrice Appleyard*
Attendants	*Joy Robson, Mollie Brown*
	Jill Gregory
Summer	*Hermione Darnborough*

ATTENDANTS	*Joan Day, Daphne Tietgen,*
	Wenda Horsburgh
AUTUMN	*Ursula Moreton*
ATTENDANTS	*Nadina Newhouse, Gwyneth Matthews,*
	Elizabeth Miller
WINTER	*Freda Bamford*
ATTENDANTS	*Anita Hill, Di Brockwell,*
	Phyllis Worthington

SINGERS	
SPRING	*Elsie Willis*
SUMMER	*Myfanwy Edwards*
AUTUMN	*Emlyn Begg*
WINTER	*George Hancock*
PHOEBUS	*Edward Holbrook*

Chorus of the Vic-Wells Opera Company

❧

THE WISE AND THE FOOLISH VIRGINS

Music by Kurt Atterberg
Scenery and costumes by William Chappell
Choreography by Ninette de Valois

First performance at Sadler's Wells Theatre
26th September, 1933

CAST

THE BRIDE	*Alicia Markova*
THE BRIDEGROOM	*Stanley Judson*
A MUSICIAN	*Claude Newman*
ANGELS	*Wenda Horsburgh, Betty Rowland*
THE WISE VIRGINS	*Hermione Darnborough, Joan Day,*
	Joy Newton, Gwyneth Matthews
LEADER	*Beatrice Appleyard*
THE FOOLISH VIRGINS	*Freda Bamford, Ailne Phillips,*
	Nadina Newhouse, Peggy Melliss
LEADER	*Sheila McCarthy*

❧

LA CREATION DU MONDE

Music by Darius Milhaud
Scenery and costumes by Edward Wolfe
Choreography by Ninette de Valois

First performance at Old Vic 30th October,
1933
(First Camargo Society performance 26th April, 1931)

CAST

THE GODS	*Maurice Brooke, Richard Ellis, John Byron*
PLANTS	*Pamela May, Wenda Horsburgh,*
	Margot Fonteyn, Daphne Tietgen
	Betty Beevor, Joan Innes

TREES	*Peggy Newton, Peggy Mellis*
ANIMALS	*Sheila McCarthy, Elizabeth Miller,*
	Molly Brown, Jill Gregory
MAN	*Anthony Tudor*
WOMAN	*Ursula Moreton*

❧

THE HAUNTED BALLROOM

Ballet in One Act

Book by Geoffrey Toye
Music by Geoffrey Toye
Scenery and costumes by Motley
Choreography by Ninette de Valois

First performance at Sadler's Wells Theatre 3rd April,
1934

CAST

THE MASTER OF TREGENNIS	*Robert Helpmann*
YOUNG TREGENNIS	*Freda Bamford*
ALICIA	*Alicia Markova*
URSULA	*Ursula Moreton*
BEATRICE	*Beatrice Appleyard*
THE STRANGER PLAYER	*William Chappell*

❧

THE JAR

After a story by Luigi Pirandello

Music by Alfred Casella
Scenery and costumes by William Chappell
Choreography by Ninette de Valois

First performed at Sadler's Wells Theatre 9th October,
1934

CAST

ZI DIMA LICASI (a mender of old china)	*Walter Gore*
DON LOLLO ZIRAFA (a rich farmer)	*Robert Helpmann*
NELA (his daughter)	*Beatrice Appleyard*
A VILLAGE BEAUTY	*Hermione Darnborough*
A YOUNG MAN WITH A GUITAR	*William Chappell*
A PEASANT	*Claude Newman*

UNCLE REMUS

Music by Gordon Jacob
Scenery and costumes by Hugh Stevenson
Choreography by Sara Patrick

First performance at Sadler's Wells Theatre 12th January,

1935

(First performance at Old Vic 19th December, 1934)

CAST

MR. BEAR	*Claude Newman*
BRER RABBIT	*Frank Staff*
UNCLE REMUS	*John Greenwood*
BRER FOX	*Joy Newton*
LITTLE BOY	*Susan Reeves*
MRS. BUZZARD	*Sheila McCarthy*
MR. TARRYPIN (Tortoise)	*Nadina Newhouse*
MR. BULLFROG	*Molly Brown*
RABBITS	*Margot Fonteyn, Jill Gregory, Joyce Haines,*
	Bernice Barry, Heather Bax, Joan Leaman

RIO GRANDE

Music by Constant Lambert
Words by Sacheverell Sitwell
Scenery and costumes by Edward Burra
Choreography by Frederick Ashton

First performed at Sadler's Wells Theatre 26th March,

1935

(First Camargo Society performance
A Day in a Southern Port
29th November, 1932)

CAST

QUEEN OF THE PORT	*Beatrice Appleyard*
STEVEDORE	*Walter Gore*
CREOLE GIRL	*Margot Fonteyn*
CREOLE BOY	*William Chappell*
WOMEN OF THE PORT	*Sheila McCarthy, Joy Newton*
	Gwyneth Matthews, Peggy Mellis,
	Pamela May, Jill Gregory,
	Wanda Horsburgh, Anne Spicer,
	Elizabeth Miller, Molly Brown
STEVEDORES, etc.	*Claude Newman, John Byron,*
	Maurice Brooke, Frank Staff,
	Leslie Edwards, Richard Ellis

CHORUS
Vic-Wells Opera Company

ALTO SOLO
Valetta Iacopi

PIANIST
Angus Morrison

THE RAKE'S PROGRESS

Ballet in Six Scenes

Music by Gavin Gordon
Scenery and costumes by Rex Whistler
Choreography by Ninette de Valois

First produced at Sadler's Wells Theatre 20th May,

1935

CAST

THE RAKE	*Walter Gore*
THE TAILOR	*Claude Newman*
THE JOCKEY	*Richard Ellis*
THE FENCING MASTER	*John Byron*
THE BRAVO	*Maurice Brooke*
THE HORNBLOWER	*Frank Staff*
THE BETRAYED GIRL	*Alicia Markova*
HER MOTHER	*Ailne Phillips*
THE DANCING MASTER	*Harold Turner*
THE DANCER	*Ursula Moreton*
THE SERVANT	*Jill Gregory*
THE RAKE'S FRIEND	*William Chappell*
THE BALLAD SINGER	*Joy Newton*
THE GENTLEMAN WITH A ROPE	*Harold Turner*
THE VIOLINIST	*John Byron*
THE SAILOR	*Claude Newman*
THE KING	*Leslie Edwards*
THE POPE	*Maurice Brooke*

GISELLE

Ballet in Two Acts

Book by Henri Vernoy de Saint-Georges, Theophile Gautier,
and Jean Coralli
Music by Adolphe Adam
Scenery and costumes by William Chappell
Choreography by Jules Perrot and Jean Coralli, reproduced
by Nicholas Sergeyev

First revived at Sadler's Wells Theatre 27th May,

1935

(First revived at Old Vic 1st January, 1934)

CAST

ALBRECHT, Duke of Silesia	*Anton Dolin*
THE PRINCE OF COURLAND	*Maurice Brooke*
WILFRID, the Duke's Squire	*Claude Newman*
HILARION, a Gamekeeper	*Walter Gore*
BATHILDE, the Duke's Fiancée	*Ursula Moreton*
BERTHE, Giselle's Mother	*Ninette de Valois*
GISLELE, a Peasant Girl	*Alicia Markova*
MYRTHA, Queen of the Wilis	*Beatrice Appleyard*
ZULME	*Margot Fonteyn*
MOYNA } Two Wilis	*Pamela May*

BAISER DE LA FEE

Music by Igor Stravinsky
(inspired by the Muse of Tchaikovsky)
Scenery and costumes by Sophie Fedorovitch
Choreography by Frederick Ashton

First performance at the Sadler's Wells Theatre
26th November, 1935

CAST

MOTHER	*Ursula Moreton*
FAIRY	*Pearl Argyle*
YOUNG MAN	*Harold Turner*
FIANCÉE	*Margot Fonteyn*

SIESTA

Music by William Walton
Miss Argyle's dress by Mattilda Etches
Choreography by Frederick Ashton

First performance at Sadler's Wells Theatre 24th January,
1936

CAST

Pearl Argyle	*Robert Helpmann*

APPARITIONS

Ballet in Five Scenes including Prologue and Epilogue

Book by Constant Lambert
Music by Franz von Liszt orchestrated by Gordon Jacob
Scenery and costumes by Cecil Beaton
Choreography by Frederick Ashton

First produced at Sadler's Wells Theatre 11th February,
1936

CAST

THE POET	*Robert Helpmann*
THE WOMAN IN BALL-DRESS	*Margot Fonteyn*
THE HUSSAR	*Harold Turner*
THE MONK	*Maurice Brooke*

THE GODS GO A-BEGGING

Ballet in One Act
Book by Sobeka (Boris Kochno)
Music by George Frederic Handel,
arranged by Sir Thomas Beecham
Scenery and costumes by Hugh Stevenson
Choreography by Ninette de Valois

First produced at Sadler's Wells Theatre 21st February,
1936

CAST

A SERVING MAID	*Elizabeth Miller*
A SHEPHERD	*William Chappell*
TWO SERVING MAIDS	*Ailne Philips, Mary Honer*
COURT LADIES	*Ursula Moreton, Beatrice Appleyard,*
	June Brae, Joy Newton, Gwyneth Matthews
NOBLEMEN	*Robert Helpmann, Harold Turner,*
	Claude Newman, John Byron,
	Leslie Edwards
BLACK LACKEYS	*Molly Brown, Joan Leaman,*
	Jill Gregory, Laurel Gill,
	Guinevere Parry, May Turner
MERCURY	*Richard Ellis*

BARABAU

Music and Words by Rieti
Scenery and costumes by Edward Burra
Choreography by Ninette de Valois

First performance at Sadler's Wells Theatre 17th April,
1936

CAST

BARABAU	*Harold Turner*
SERGEANT	*Frederick Ashton*
PEASANT WOMAN	*Ninette de Valois*

CHORUS

Vic-Wells Opera Company

PROMETHEUS

Music by Beethoven, arranged by Constant Lambert
Scenery and costumes by John Bantry
Choreography by Ninette de Valois

First performance at Sadler's Wells Theatre
3rd November, 1936

CAST

PROMETHEUS	*Robert Helpmann*
HIS WIFE	*Ninette de Valois*
THE OTHER WOMAN	*Pamela May*
THE FRIEND	*Harold Turner*

NOCTURNE

Ballet in One Act

Music by Frederick Delius
Scenery and costumes by Sophie Fedorovich
Choreography by Frederick Ashton

First produced at Sadler's Wells Theatre 10th November, 1936

CAST

A SPECTATOR	*Frederick Ashton*
A YOUNG MAN	*Robert Helpmann*
A RICH GIRL	*June Brae*
A POOR GIRL	*Margot Fonteyn*

❧

CASSE-NOISETTE

Ballet in Two Acts

Music by Piotr Ilich Tchaikovsky
Scenery and costumes by Mtislav Dobouzhinsky
Choreography by Lev Ivanov, reproduced by Nicholas Sergeyev

First revived in entirety at Sadler's Wells Theatre 8th January, 1937[1]

CAST

PRESIDENT	*Maurice Brooke*
HIS WIFE	*Ursula Moreton*
FRITZ } their children	*Jean Bedells*
CLARA }	*June Vincent*
DROSSELMEYER	*Claude Newman*
AUNT MARIANNA	*Sheila McCarthy*
GOVERNESS	*Wenda Horsburgh*
BUTLER	*John Greenwood*
MECHANICAL DOLLS:	
VIVANDIERE	*Laurel Martyn*
SOLDIER	*Guinevere Parry*
COLUMBINE	*Molly Brown*
HARLEQUIN	*Don Burrows*
KING OF MICE	*Don Burrows*
NUTCRACKER	*Deryk Mendel*
CHOCOLAT: Danse Espagnole	*Ailne Phillips, Harold Turner*
CAFE: Danse Arabe	*Maurice Brooke, Leslie Edwards, Paul Reyloff*
THE: Danse Chinois	*William Chappell, Michael Somes*
BOUFFON	*Claude Newman*
DANSE DES MIRLITONS	*Jill Gregory, Laurel Martyn, Guinevere Parry, Julia Farron*
PAS DE DEUX	*Margot Fonteyn, Robert Helpmann*
THE SUGAR-PLUM FAIRY	*Margot Fonteyn*

[1] This ballet was first revived by the "Wells" Company at the Sadler's Wells Theatre on 30th January, 1934, with scenery and costumes by Hedley Briggs. The roles of the Sugar-Plum Fairy and her cavalier were danced by Alicia Markova and Harold Turner.

LES PATINEURS

Ballet in One Act

Music by Meyerbeer, arranged by Constant Lambert
Scenery and costumes by William Chappell
Choreography by Frederick Ashton

First produced at Sadler's Wells Theatre 16th February, 1937

CAST

ENTREE	*Mary Honer, Elizabeth Miller*
PAS DE HUIT	*Gwyneth Matthews, Joy Newton, Peggy Melliss, Wenda Horsburgh, Richard Ellis, Leslie Edwards, Michael Somes, Paul Reyloff*
VARIATION	*Harold Turner*
PAS DE DEUX	*Margot Fonteyn, Robert Helpmann*
ENSEMBLE	*Margot Fonteyn, Mary Honer, Elizabeth Miller, Pamela May, June Brae*
PAS DE HUIT	*The same with Harold Turner and Robert Helpmann*
PAS DE TROIS	*Mary Honer, Elizabeth Miller, Harold Turner*
PAS DES PATINEUSES	*June Brae, Pamela May*
ENSEMBLE	*Mary Honer, Elizabeth Miller, Pamela May, June Brae, Harold Turner, Richard Ellis, Leslie Edwards, Michael Somes, Paul Reyloff*

❧

WEDDING BOUQUET

Words by Gertrude Stein
Music by Lord Berners
Scenery and costumes by Lord Berners
Choreography by Frederick Ashton

First performance at Sadler's Wells Theatre, 27th April, 1937

CAST

BRIDE	*Mary Honer*
BRIDEGROOM	*Robert Helpmann*
JOSEPHINE	*June Brae*
VIOLET	*Pamela May*
THERESE	*Elizabeth Miller*
JULIA	*Margot Fonteyn*
JULIA'S DOG, PEPE	*Julia Farron*
WEBSTER	*Ninette de Valois*
PAUL	*Harold Turner*
JOHN	*William Chappell*
ERNEST	*Ernest Newman*
ARTHUR	*Leslie Edwards*
GUY	*Michael Somes*
ORATOR	*Constant Lambert*

CHECKMATE

Ballet in One Scene with Prologue

Music by *Arthur Bliss*
Scenery and costumes by *E. McKnight Kauffer*
Choreography by *Ninette de Valois*
First produced at Théâtre des Champs-Élysées, Paris,
1st June, 1937

CAST

Two Chess Players	*Frederick Ashton, Alan Carter*
Red Pawns	*Jill Gregory, Molly Brown,*
	Linda Sheridan, Laurel Martyn,
	Elizabeth Kennedy, Joan Leaman,
	Wenda Horsburgh, Julia Farron
First Red Knight	*Harold Turner*
Second Red Knight	*William Chappell*
Black Knights	*Richard Ellis, Michael Somes*
The Black Queen	*June Brae*
The Red King	*Robert Helpmann*
The Red Queen	*Pamela May*
Red Castles	*Leslie Edwards, John Nicholson*
Red Bishops	*Claude Newman, Paul Reyloff*
Black Pawns	*Margot Fonteyn, Mary Honer,*
	Elizabeth Miller, Pamela May
Black Castles	*Joy Newton, Anne Spicer*

LES RENDEZ-VOUS

Ballet in One Scene

Music by *Daniel François Auber,*
arranged by Constant Lambert
Scenery and costumes by *William Chappell*
Choreography by *Frederick Ashton*

First produced with present setting and costumes at
Sadler's Wells Theatre 16th November, 1937

CAST

Pas de Quatre	*Molly Brown, Guinevere Parry,*
	Julia Farron, Laurel Martyn
Variation	*Harold Turner*
Adagio of Lovers	*Margot Fonteyn, Harold Turner*
Pas de Trois	*Jill Gregory, Frederick Ashton,*
	Claude Newman
Pas de Six	*Claude Newman, Leslie Edwards,*
	Richard Ellis, Michael Somes,
	Paul Reymond, Alan Carter

HOROSCOPE

Ballet in One Act

Book by *Constant Lambert*
Music by *Constant Lambert*
Scenery and costumes by *Sophie Fedorovitch*
Choreography by *Frederick Ashton*
First produced at Sadler's Wells Theatre 27th January,
1938

CAST

The Young Man (Sun in Leo, Moon in Gemini)	*Michael Somes*
The Young Woman (Sun in Virgo, Moon in Gemini)	*Margot Fonteyn*
The Gemini	*Richard Ellis, Alan Carter*
The Moon	*Pamela May*

LE ROI NU

(The Emperor's New Clothes)

Scenario by *Serge Lifar after Hans Andersen*
Music by *Jean Françaix*
Scenery and costumes by *Hedley Briggs*
Choreography by *Ninette de Valois*

First performance at Sadler's Wells Theatre 7th April,
1938

CAST

The Emperor	*Robert Helpmann*
The Empress	*Pearl Argyle*
The Empress's Lover	*Harold Turner*
First Tailor	*Frederick Ashton*
Second Tailor	*William Chappell*
Third Tailor	*Claude Newman*
Serving Maids	*Joy Newton, Linda Sheridan,*
	Wenda Horsburgh
Three Ministers	*Michael Somes, Alan Carter,*
	Stanley Hall
Two Peasants	*Mary Honer, Harold Turner*
A Child	*Margaret Dale*
Guards	*Leslie Edwards, David Gray,*
	John Nicholson
Pages	*Molly Brown, Jill Gregory,*
	Julia Farron, Guinevere Parry,
	Mavis Jackson, Rowena Fayre

PEASANTS   *Joy Newton, Linda Sheridan,*
Wenda Horsburgh, Anne Spicer,
Joan Leaman, Annabel Farjeon,
Elizabeth Kennedy, Palma Nye,
Patricia Bulman, Betty Cotton,
Valerie Wade, Rose Bayly,
Leslie Edwards, David Grey,
Paul Reymond, John Nicholson

THE JUDGMENT OF PARIS

Music by Lennox Berkeley
Scenery and costumes by William Chappell
Choreography by Frederick Ashton

First performance at Sadler's Wells Theatre 10th May,
1938

CAST

PARIS	*Robert Helpmann*
VENUS	*Pearl Argyle*
JUNO	*Elizabeth Miller*
MINERVA	*Mary Honer*
MERCURY	*William Chappell*

HARLEQUIN IN THE STREET

Music by Couperin
Scenery and costumes by André Derain
Choreography by Frederick Ashton

First performance Sadler's Wells Theatre 10th November,
1938

CAST

LA SUPERBE	*June Brae*
MONSEIGNEUR	*Michael Somes*
HARLEQUIN	*Alan Carter*
PORTERS	*Stanley Hall, John Hart*
COMMÉRES	*Palma Nye, Jill Gregory,*
	Patricia Garnett
BIRDCATCHER	*Richard Ellis*
BREAD BOY	*Frank Staff*
LETTER BEARER	*John Nicholson*

THE SLEEPING PRINCESS

Ballet in three Acts and a Prologue

Music by Piotr Ilich Tchaikovsky
Scenery and costumes by Nadia Benois
Choreography by Marius Petipa
Reproduced by Nicholas Sergeyev

First revived in entirety at Sadler's Wells Theatre
2nd February, 1939

CAST

KING FLORESTAN XXIV	*Bruce Dargavel*
THE QUEEN	*Joy Newton*
CATALBUTTE (Master of Ceremonies)	*Carol Bertram*
THE CAMELIA FAIRY	*Palma Nye*
HER CAVALIER	*Leslie Edwards*
THE ROSE FAIRY	*Pamela May*
HER CAVALIER	*Richard Ellis*
THE VIOLET FAIRY	*Mary Honer*
HER CAVALIER	*William Chappell*
THE FAIRY OF THE SONG BIRDS	*Elizabeth Miller*
HER CAVALIER	*Frank Staff*
THE BREADCRUMB FAIRY	*Julia Farron*
HER CAVALIER	*Alan Carter*
THE LILAC FAIRY	*June Brae*
HER CAVALIER	*Michael Somes*
CARABOSSE (The Wicked Fairy)	*John Greenwood*
PRINCESS AURORA	*Margot Fonteyn*
FIRST PRINCE	*Harold Turner*
SECOND PRINCE	*Frederick Ashton*
THIRD PRINCE	*William Chappell*
FOURTH PRINCE	*Frank Staff*
COUNTESS	*Ursula Moreton*
PRINCE CHARMING	*Robert Helpmann*
GALLISSON (The Prince's Tutor)	*Claude Newman*
A VISION OF THE PRINCESS AURORA	*Margot Fonteyn*
THE DIAMOND FAIRY	*Pamela May*
THE GOLD FAIRY	*Jill Gregory*
THE SILVER FAIRY	*Patricia Garnett*
THE SAPPHIRE FAIRY	*Julia Farron*
PUSS IN BOOTS AND THE WHITE CAT	*Frederick Ashton, Molly Brown*
THE PRINCESS FLORISSE	*Mary Honer*
THE BLUE BIRD	*Harold Turner*
RED RIDING HOOD AND THE WOLF	*Jean Bedells, Frank Staff*
CINDERELLA	*Ursula Moreton*
PRINCE FORTUNE	*Richard Ellis*

CUPID AND PSYCHE

Music by Lord Berners
Scenery and costumes by Sir Francis Rose
Choreography by Frederick Ashton
First performance at Sadler's Wells Theatre 27th April,
1939

CAST

TANAGRA WOMEN	*Valerie Wade, Moyra Fraser,*
	Margaret Williams,
	Stella Villiers-Stuart
PAN	*Michael Somes*
NYMPHS	*Palma Nye, Joan Leaman*
TOWNSPEOPLE	*Joy Newton, Anne Spicer, Anabel Farjeon,*
	Patricia Garnett, Joan Ross,
	Audrey Daglish, William Chappell,
	Claude Newman, Paul Reymond,
	John Nicholson, Stanley Hall
PSYCHE	*Julia Farron*
CUPID	*Frank Staff*
VENUS	*June Brae*
ATTENDANTS ON VENUS	*Molly Brown, Guinevere Parry,*
	Rowena Tayre, Margaret Dale

☙

LES SYLPHIDES

Ballet in One Act

Music by Frederic Chopin
orchestrated by Gordon Jacob
Scenery and costumes after Alexandre Benois
Choreography by Michel Fokine
First revived at Sadler's Wells Theatre 26th December,
1939

CAST

NOCTURNE	*Margot Fonteyn, Mary Honer, Pamela May,*
	Robert Helpmann, Jill Gregory,
	Jean Bedells, Guinevere Parry,
	Joy Newton, Anne Spicer,
	Elizabeth Kennedy, Joan Leaman,
	Mavis Jackson, Patricia Garnett,
	Palma Nye, Olive Deacon, Joan Ross,
	Margaret Dale, Annabel Farjeon,
	Joan Phillips, June Vincent
VALSE	*Mary Honer*
MAZURKA	*Margot Fonteyn*
MAZURKA	*Robert Helpmann*
PRELUDE	*Pamela May*
VALSE	*Margot Fonteyn, Robert Helpmann*
GRANDE VALSE (Finale)	*Margot Fonteyn, Mary Honer,*
	Pamela May, Robert Helpmann
	and ensemble

DANTE SONATA

Ballet in one Act

Music by Liszt, orchestrated by Constant Lambert
Scenery and costumes by Sophie Fedorovich after Flaxman
Choreography by Frederick Ashton
First produced Sadler's Wells Theatre 23rd January,
1940

CAST

Margot Fonteyn, Pamela May, Julia Farron, Anne Spicer,
Olive Deacon, Joan Phillips, Joan Leaman, Margaret Dale,
Michael Somes, Richard Ellis, Leslie Edwards, Leo Young.

June Brae, Joy Newton, Patricia Garnett, Palma Nye,
Guinevere Parry, Mavis Jackson, Annabel Farjeon,
Joan Ross, Robert Helpmann, Alan Carter, John Hart,
Stanley Hall

☙

COPPELIA

Ballet in Two Acts

Book by Charles Nuitter and Arthur Saint-Leon
Music by Leo Delibes
Scenery and costumes by William Chappell
Choreography by Lev Ivanov and Enrico Cecchetti
Reproduced by Nicholas Sergeyev

First revived with present setting by " Wells " Company,
Sadler's Wells Theatre, 15th April, 1940[1]

CAST

SWANILDA	*Mary Honer*
FRANZ	*Robert Helpmann*
DR. COPPELIUS (a toymaker)	*Claude Newman*
BURGOMASTER	*John Greenwood*
COPPELIA	*Bunty Kelley*
THE DUKE	*Leslie Edwards*
DAWN	*Pamela May*
PRAYER	*June Brae*
HYMEN	*Ursula Moreton, Richard Ellis*

[1] This ballet was first revived by the "Wells" company at the Sadler's Wells Theatre on 21st March, 1933 with scenery and costumes by Edwin Calligan. The principal roles of Swanilda and Coppelius were taken by Lydia Lopokova and Hedley Briggs.

THE WISE VIRGINS

Ballet in One Act

Music by Johann Sebastian Bach
orchestrated by William Walton
Scenery and costumes by Rex Whistler
Choreography by Frederick Ashton

First produced at Sadler's Wells Theatre 24th April,
1940

CAST

THE BRIDEGROOM	*Michael Somes*
THE BRIDE	*Margot Fonteyn*
THE FATHER	*Claude Newman*
HER MOTHER	*Annabel Farjeon*
WISE VIRGINS	*Julia Farron, Olive Deacon,*
	Joan Leaman, Joan Phillips, Palma Nye
FOOLISH VIRGINS	*Mary Honer, Elizabeth Kennedy,*
	Joy Newton, Patricia Garnett,
	Jean Bedells
ANGELS	*Richard Ellis, John Hart,*
	Leslie Edwards, Leo Young, Stanley Hall
CHERUBS	*Deryk Mendel, Margaret Dale,*
	Guinevere Parry, Mavis Jackson

❧

THE PROSPECT BEFORE US

Ballet in Seven Scenes

Book by Ninette de Valois
Music by William Boyce, arranged by Constant Lambert
Scenery and costumes by Roger Furse
Choreography by Ninette de Valois

First produced at Sadler's Wells Theatre 4th July,
1940

CAST

MR. TAYLOR (Manager of the King's Theatre)	*Claude Newman*
MR. O'REILLY (Manager of the Pantheon)	*Robert Helpmann*
MONSIEUR NOVERRE (Choreographer and Ballet Master)	*Frederick Ashton*
MADAME NOVERRE	*Ursula Moreton*
MADEMOISELLE THEODORE (Première Danseuse)	*Pamela May*
MONSIEUR DIDELOT	*Alan Carter*
MONSIEUR VESTRIS	*John Hart*

LADIES OF THE BALLET	*Julia Farron, Palma Nye,*
	Joy Newton, Wenda Horsburgh,
	Elizabeth Kennedy, Joan Ross,
	Margaret Williams, Moyra Fraser
PATRONS OF THE BALLET	*Anne Spicer, Leo Young*
	Stanley Hall
TWO DANCERS	*Molly Brown, Patricia Garnett*
THE DRUMS	*Leo Young*
THE HORN	*Paul Reymond*
A DANCER	*Mary Honer*
CUPID	*Margaret Dale*
MR. TAYLOR'S LAWYERS	*Michael Somes, Richard Ellis,*
	Leslie Edwards
THREE NOBLE LORDS	*Paul Reymond, Stanley Hall,*
	Leo Young

❧

FAÇADE

Ballet in One Act

Freely adapted from poems by Edith Sitwell
Music by William Walton
Scenery and costumes by John Armstrong
Choreography by Frederick Ashton

First produced at Sadler's Wells Theatre 23rd July,
1940

CAST

SCOTCH RHAPSODY	*Guinevere Parry, Molly Brown*
	Claude Newman
NOCHE ESPAGNOLE	*Frederick Ashton*
YODELLING SONG :	
THE MILK MAID	*Julia Farron*
MOUNTAINEERS	*Michael Somes, John Hart,*
	Richard Ellis
POLKA	*Margot Fonteyn*
FOXTROT	*June Brae, Pamela May,*
	Robert Helpmann, Frederick Ashton
WALTZ	*Anne Spicer, Julia Farron,*
	Palma Nye, Moyra Fraser
POPULAR SONG	*Richard Ellis, John Hart*
COUNTRY DANCE :	
A MAIDEN	*Mary Honer*
A YOKEL	*Michael Somes*
THE SQUIRE	*Robert Helpmann*
TANGO :	
A DAGO	*Frederick Ashton*
A DEBUTANTE	*Margot Fonteyn*

THE WANDERER

Choreographic Fantasy in Four Scenes

Book by Frederick Ashton
Music by Franz Peter Schubert
Scenery and costumes by Graham Sutherland
Choreography by Frederick Ashton

First produced at the New Theatre, London,
27th January, 1941

CAST

ALLEGRO CON FUOCO   *Robert Helpmann, Alan Carter,*
John Hart, Leslie Edwards, John Field,
Margot Fonteyn, Mary Honer,
Patricia Garnett, Julia Farron,
Pamela May, Michael Somes

ADAGIO   *Robert Helpmann, Joy Newton,*
Palma Nye, Wenda Horsburgh,
Guinevere Parry, Joan Phillips,
Elizabeth Kennedy, Alan Carter,
John Hart, Leslie Edwards,
John Field, Julia Farron,
Margaret Dale, Deryk Mendel

PRESTO   *Robert Helpmann, Mary Honer,*
Patricia Garnett, Margot Fonteyn,
Alan Carter, John Hart,
Leslie Edwards, John Field,
Pamela May, Michael Somes

☙

COMUS

Masque in One Act, after Milton

Music by Henry Purcell, arranged by Constant Lambert
Scenery and costumes by Oliver Messel
Choreography by Robert Helpmann

First produced at New Theatre, London, 26th March,
1941

CAST

ATTENDANT SPIRIT   *Margaret Dale*
COMUS   *Robert Helpmann*
THE LADY   *Margot Fonteyn*
HER BROTHERS   *John Hart, David Paltenghi*
SABRINA   *Moyra Fraser*

ORPHEUS AND EURYDICE

Ballet in Two Acts

Book after R. de' Calzabizi
Music by Christoph Willibald von Gluck
Scenery and costumes by Sophie Fedorovitch
Choreography by Ninette de Valois

First produced at New Theatre, London, 28th May,
1941

CAST

ORPHEUS   *Robert Helpmann*
LOVE   *Margot Fonteyn*
LEADER OF THE FURIES   *Mary Honer*
PEASANTS   *John Hart, Julia Farron*

☙

HAMLET

Ballet in One Scene

Music by Piotr Ilich Tchaikovsky
Scenery and costumes by Leslie Hurry
Choreography by Robert Helpmann

First produced at the New Theatre, London, 19th May,
1942

CAST

KING OF DENMARK   *David Paltenghi*
HAMLET (Son of the late King,
   Nephew to the present King)   *Robert Helpmann*
POLONIUS (Lord Chamberlain)   *Gordon Hamilton*
LAERTES (Son to Polonius)   *John Hart*
GRAVE-DIGGER   *Leo Kersley*
GHOST OF HAMLET'S FATHER   *Alexis Rassine*
QUEEN OF DENMARK (and Mother
   to Hamlet)   *Celia Franca*
OPHELIA (Daughter to Polonius)   *Margot Fonteyn*
PAGE   *Margaret Dale*

☙

THE BIRDS

Music by Ottorino Respighi
Scenery and costumes by Chiang Yee
Choreography by Robert Helpmann

First performance at New Theatre, London,
24th November, 1942

CAST

CUCKOO   *Gordon Hamilton*
SPARROWS   *Margaret Dale, Joan Sheldon*
NIGHTINGALE   *Beryl Grey*
DOVE   *Alexis Rassine*
DOVE'S ATTENDANTS   *Anne Lascelles, Moira Shearer*
Pauline Clayden, Lorna Mossford
HEN   *Moyra Fraser*

THE QUEST

Ballet in Five Scenes

Book by Doris Langley Moore
after Spenser's " Faerie Queene "
Music by William Walton
Scenery and costumes by John Piper
Choreography by Frederick Ashton

First produced at the New Theatre, London, 7th April,
1943

CAST

ARCHIMAGO (a Magician personifying Hypocrisy)	*Leslie Edwards*
FEMALE SERVANT (transformed into Una)	*Celia Franca*
MALE SERVANT	*Anthony Burke*
BATS (Evil Spirits)	*Pauline Clayden, Lorna Mossford*
ST. GEORGE (the Red Cross Knight, personifying Holiness)	*Robert Helpmann*
UNA (personifying Truth)	*Margot Fonteyn*
SANSFOY (Faithless)	*Franklin White*
SANSJOY (Joyless)	*David Paltenghi*
DUESSA (personifying Falsehood)	*Beryl Grey*
SANSLOY (Lawless)	*Alexis Rassine*
SLOTH	*Nigel Desmond*
GLUTTONY	*Ray Powell*
WRATH	*Celia Franca*
LECHERY	*Anthony Burke*
AVARICE	*Gordon Hamilton*
ENVY	*Palma Nye*
PRIDE (as Queen)	*Moira Shearer*
FAITH	*Julia Farron*
CHARITY	*Jean Bedells*
HOPE	*Moyra Fraser*

❧

LE LAC DES CYGNES

Ballet in Four Acts

Book by V. P. Begitchev and Geltser
Music by Piotr Ilich Tchaikovsky
Scenery and costumes by Leslie Hurry
Choreography by Marius Petipa and Lev Ivanov,
Reproduced by Nicholas Sergeyev

Revived at New Theatre, London, 7th September,
1943[1]

CAST

PRINCE SIEGFRIED	*Robert Helpmann*
THE PRINCESS MOTHER	*Joy Newton*
WOLFGANG (Tutor to the Prince)	*Ray Powell*
BENNO (The Prince's Friend)	*Leslie Edwards*
ODETTE (The Swan Queen)	*Margot Fonteyn*
A PEASANT GIRL	*Jill Gregory*
CYGNETS	*Joan Sheldon, Pauline Clayden, Jill Gregory, Elizabeth Kennedy*
TWO SWANS	*Celia Franca, Palma Nye*
VON ROTHBART (an evil Magician)	*Nigel Desmond*
ODILE (his Daughter)	*Margot Fonteyn*
COURT LADIES	*Elizabeth Kennedy, Lorna Mossford, Mavis Jackson, Moyra Fraser, Moira Shearer, Paula Dunning*
PAS DE TROIS	*Alexis Rassine, Margaret Dale, Joan Sheldon*
SPANISH DANCE	*Celia Franca, Palma Nye*
CZARDAS	*Peggy van Praagh, June Vincent, Gordon Hamilton, Ray Powell*
MAZURKA	*Wenda Horsburgh, Julia Farron, Jill Gregory, Jean Bedells, Franklin White, Anthony Burke, Leslie Edwards, Philip Chatfield*

[1] This ballet was first revived by the " Wells " Company at the Sadler's
Wells Theatre on 20th November, 1934, with scenery and costumes by
Hugh Stevenson. The principal roles of Odette-Odile and Prince Siegfried
were then taken by Alicia Markova and Robert Helpmann respectively.

❧

LE SPECTRE DE LA ROSE

Ballet in One Act

Book by J. L. Vaudoyer
Music by Carl von Weber
Scenery and costumes by Rex Whistler
Choreography after Michel Fokine

Revived New Theatre, London, 1st February,
1944

CAST

THE YOUNG GIRL	*Margot Fonteyn*
THE SPIRIT OF THE ROSE	*Alexis Rassine*

❧

THE SPIDER'S BANQUET

Ballet in One Act

Book by Gilbert de Voisins
Music by Albert Roussel
Scenery and costumes by Michael Ayrton
Choreography by Andrée Howard

First produced at the New Theatre, London, 20th June,
1944

THE SPIDER	Celia Franca
ANTS	Joan Sheldon, Jill Gregory, Anne Negus,
	Guinevere Parry, Elizabeth Kennedy,
	Joan Valerie, Avril Navarre,
	Gillian Lynne
BEETLES	Rosemary Lindsay, Paula Dunning
THE BUTTERFLY	Moira Shearer
GRUBS	Mavis Jackson, June Vincent
PRAYING MANTISES	Gordon Hamilton, Ray Powell
THE MAYFLY	Pauline Clayden
THE DRAGONFLY	Henry Danton

LE CARNAVAL

Ballet in One Act

Book by Michel Fokine
Music by Robert Schumann
Scenery and costumes after Leon Bakst
Choreography after Michel Fokine

First revived at Princes Theatre, London, 10th October,
1944

CAST

COLUMBINE	Margot Fonteyn
CHIARINA	Pamela May
ESTRELLA	Julia Farron
PAPILLON	Pauline Clayden
HARLEQUIN	Alexis Rassine
PIERROT	Robert Helpmann
EUSEBIUS	David Paltenghi
PANTALON	Gordon Hamilton
FLORESTAN	Leslie Edwards

PROMENADE

Music by Franz Joseph Haydn, arranged by Edwin Evans
Scenery and costumes by Hugh Stevenson
Choreography by Ninette de Valois

First produced Kings Theatre, Edinburgh, 25th October,
1944

CAST

THE LEPIDOPTERIST	Gordon Hamilton
ENTREE	Joan Sheldon, Margaret Dale, Anne Lascelles,
	Guinevere Parry, Wenda Horsburgh
LES MERVEILLEUSES	Julia Farron, Jean Bedells,
	Moyra Fraser, Leslie Edwards
RENDEZ-VOUS	Beryl Grey, David Paltenghi
PROMENADE	Pauline Clayden
PAS DE TROIS	Moira Shearer, Alexis Rassine,
	Ray Powell

MIRACLE IN THE GORBALS

Ballet in One Act

Music by Arthur Bliss
Scenery and costumes by Edward Burra
Choreography by Robert Helpmann

First produced at Prince's Theatre, London, 26th October,
1944

CAST

THE SUICIDE	Pauline Clayden
THE LOVERS	Moira Shearer, Alexis Rassine
A BEGGAR	Leslie Edwards
A STREET BOY	Gordon Hamilton
THE OFFICIAL	David Paltenghi
THE PROSTITUTE	Celia Franca
THE STRANGER	Robert Helpmann

The Sadler's Wells Ballet—Covent Garden

1946-1955

THE SLEEPING BEAUTY

Ballet with Three Acts and a Prologue
Music by Piotr Ilich Tchaikovsky
Scenery and costumes by Oliver Messel
Choreography by Marius Petipa
Produced by Nicholas Sergeyev

First performance at Covent Garden 20th February,
1946

CAST

KING FLORESTAN XXIV	*David Davenport*
HIS QUEEN	*Julia Farron*
CATTALABUTTE (Master of Ceremonies)	*Leslie Edwards*
FAIRY OF THE CRYSTAL FOUNTAIN	*Moira Shearer*
HER CAVALIER	*Alexis Rassine*
FAIRY OF THE ENCHANTED GARDEN	*Gillian Lynne*
HER CAVALIER	*Henry Danton*
FAIRY OF THE WOODLAND GLADES	*Anne Negus*
HER CAVALIER	*Harold Turner*
FAIRY OF THE SONG BIRDS	*Pauline Clayden*
HER CAVALIER	*Richard Ellis*
FAIRY OF THE GOLDEN VINE	*Margaret Dale*
HER CAVALIER	*Franklin White*
FAIRY OF THE LILAC	*Beryl Grey*
HER CAVALIER	*Michael Somes*
CARABOSSE (The Wicked Fairy)	*Robert Helpmann*
THE PRINCESS AURORA	*Margot Fonteyn*
THE FIRST PRINCE	*Harold Turner*
THE SECOND PRINCE	*Anthony Burke*
THE THIRD PRINCE	*Henry Danton*
THE FOURTH PRINCE	*Richard Ellis*
PRINCE FLORIMUND	*Robert Helpmann*
THE COUNTESS	*Jean Bedells*
GALLISON (The Prince's Tutor)	*Paul Reymond*
A VISION OF PRINCESS AURORA	*Margot Fonteyn*
BLUEBEARD AND HIS WIFE	*Norman Thomson, Margaret Roseby*
GOLDILOCKS AND HER PRINCE	*Paula Dunning, Paul Reymond*
BEAUTY AND THE BEAST	*Christine du Boulay, Toni Repetto*
FLORESTAN AND HIS TWO SISTERS	*Michael Somes, Moira Shearer, Gerd Larsen*
PUSS-IN-BOOTS and THE WHITE CAT	*Stanley Holden, Margaret Dale*
THE BLUE BIRDS	*Pamela May, Alexis Rassine*
RED RIDING HOOD AND THE WOLF	*June Leighton, Richard Ellis*
THE THREE IVANS	*Harold Turner, Gordon Hamilton, Franklin White*

❧

THE RAKE'S PROGRESS

Ballet in Six Scenes
Ballet by Gavin Gordon after William Hogarth
Music by Gavin Gordon
Scenery and costumes by Rex Whistler after William Hogarth
Choreography by Ninette de Valois

First produced at Covent Garden 18th March,
1946

CAST

THE RAKE	*Robert Helpmann*
THE TAILOR	*Claude Newman*
THE JOCKEY	*Franklin White*
THE BRAVO	*Anthony Burke*
THE DANCING MASTER	*Gordon Hamilton*
THE FENCING MASTER	*David Paltenghi*
THE HORNBLOWER	*Leslie Edwards*
THE BETRAYED GIRL	*Margot Fonteyn*
HER MOTHER	*Elizabeth Kennedy*
THE DANCER	*Moira Shearer*
THE RAKE'S FRIEND	*Alexis Rassine*
THE BALLAD SINGER	*Joy Newton*
THE SERVANT	*June Leighton*
THE GENTLEMAN WITH A ROPE	*Gordon Hamilton*
THE SAILOR	*Franklin White*
THE CARD PLAYER	*Alexis Rassine*
THE VIOLINIST	*David Paltenghi*
THE KING	*Toni Repetto*
THE POPE	*Stanley Hall*

NOCTURNE

Ballet in One Act

Music by Frederick Delius
Scenery and costumes by Sophie Fedorovitch
Choreography by Frederick Ashton
First produced at Covent Garden 18th March,
1946

CAST

A SPECTATOR	*Frederick Ashton*
A YOUNG GIRL	*Pamela May*
A FLOWER GIRL	*Margot Fonteyn*
A YOUNG MAN	*Robert Helpmann*

MIRACLE IN THE GORBALS

Ballet in One Act

Music by Arthur Bliss
Scenario by Michael Benthall
Scenery and costumes by Edward Burra
Choreography by Robert Helpmann
First produced at Covent Garden 18th March,
1946

CAST

THE SUICIDE	*Pauline Clayden*
THE LOVERS	*Moira Shearer, Alexis Rassine*
A BEGGAR	*Leslie Edwards*
A STREET BOY	*Gordon Hamilton*
THE OFFICIAL	*David Paltenghi*
THE PROSTITUTE	*Julia Farron*
THE STRANGER	*Robert Helpmann*

DANTE SONATA

Ballet in One Act

Music by Liszt, orchestrated by Constant Lambert
Scenery and Costumes by Sophie Fedorovitch, after Flaxman
Choreography by Frederick Ashton
First produced at Covent Garden 20th March,
1946

CAST

CHILDREN OF LIGHT:
*Margot Fonteyn, Pamela May, Moira Shearer, Julia Farron,
Margaret Dale, Gerd Larsen, Joan Sheldon, Gillian Lynne,
David Paltenghi, Henry Danton, Leslie Edwards,
Kenneth Melville*

CHILDREN OF DARKNESS:
*Beryl Grey, Palma Nye, Jill Gregory, Guinevere Parry,
Elizabeth Kennedy, Avril Navarre, Paula Dunning,
Anne Negus, Robert Helpmann, Anthony Burke,
Franklin White, Brian Shaw*

LES PATINEURS

Ballet in One Act

Music by Meyerbeer, arranged by Constant Lambert
Scenery and costumes by William Chappell
Choreography by Frederick Ashton
First produced at Covent Garden 20th March,
1946

CAST

ENTREE	*Margaret Dale, Avril Navarre*
PAS-DE-HUIT	*Jill Gregory, Margaret Roseby,*
	Oenone Talbot, Margaret Sear,
	Henry Danton, Franklin White,
	Brian Shaw, Kenneth Melville
VARIATION	*Harold Turner*
PAS-DE-DEUX	*Moira Shearer, David Paltenghi*
ENSEMBLE	*Beryl Grey, Gillian Lynne,*
	Harold Turner, Margaret Dale,
	Avril Navarre and Pas-de-Huit
PAS-DE-TROIS	*Margaret Dale, Avril Navarre,*
	Harold Turner
PAS-DES-PATINEUSES	*Beryl Grey, Gillian Lynne*
ENSEMBLE	*Beryl Grey, Gillian Lynne,*
	Margaret Dale, Avril Navarre,
	Henry Danton, Franklin White,
	Brian Shaw, Kenneth Melville

ADAM ZERO

Ballet in One Act by Michael Benthall

Music by Arthur Bliss
Scenery and costumes by Roger Furse
Choreography by Robert Helpmann
First performance Covent Garden 10th April,
1946

CAST

THE STAGE DIRECTOR	*David Paltenghi*
THE CHOREOGRAPHER	
(Creator and Destroyer)	*June Brae*
THE PRINCIPAL DANCER (Adam Zero)	*Robert Helpmann*

THE DESIGNER	*Jean Bedells*
THE WARDROBE MISTRESS }(His fates)	*Julia Farron*
THE DRESSER	*Palma Nye*
THE BALLERINA (His first love, wife and mistress)	*June Brae*
THE UNDERSTUDIES (His son and daughter)	*Alexis Rassine, Gillian Lynne*
THE CHARACTER DANCERS (His cat and dog)	*Pauline Clayden, Gordon Hamilton*
THE MIME (His spiritual adviser)	*Leslie Edwards*

❧

SYMPHONIC VARIATIONS

Music by Cesar Franck
Scenery and costumes by Sophie Fedorovitch
Choreography by Frederick Ashton

First performance Covent Garden 24th April, 1946

CAST

Margot Fonteyn	*Michael Somes*
Pamela May	*Brian Shaw*
Moira Shearer	*Henry Danton*

❧

LES SYLPHIDES

Music by Frederic Chopin
orchestrated by Gordon Jacob
Scenery and costumes after designs by Alexandre Benois
Choreography by Michel Fokine

First produced at Covent Garden 15th May, 1946

CAST

NOCTURNE	*Margot Fonteyn, Alexis Rassine, Moira Shearer, Anne Negus, Margaret Dale, Jill Gregory, June Leighton, Guinevere Parry, Avril Navarre, Elizabeth Kennedy, Margaret Sear, Oenone Talbot, Joan Sheldon, Anne Gieves, Mavis Spence, Christine du Boulay, Margaret Roseby, Rosemary Lindsay, Lorna Mossford, Gillian Lynne*
VALSE	*Anne Negus*
MAZURKA	*Margot Fonteyn*
MAZURKA	*Alexis Rassine*
PRELUDE	*Moira Shearer*
PAS DE DEUX	*Margot Fonteyn, Alexis Rassine*
FINALE	*Ensemble*

HAMLET

Ballet in One Scene

Music by Piotr Ilich Tchaikovsky
Scenery and costumes by Leslie Hurry
Choreography by Robert Helpmann

First produced at Covent Garden 3rd June, 1946

CAST

KING OF DENMARK	*Anthony Burke*
HAMLET (Son of the late King, Nephew to the present King)	*David Paltenghi*
POLONIUS (Lord Chamberlain)	*Paul Reymond*
LAERTES (Son to Polonius)	*Michael Somes,*
GRAVEDIGGER	*Harold Turner*
GHOST OF HAMLET'S FATHER	*Leslie Edwards*
QUEEN OF DENMARK AND MOTHER TO HAMLET	*Beryl Grey*
OPHELIA (Daughter to Polonius)	*Margot Fonteyn*
PAGE	*Margaret Dale*

GISELLE

Ballet in Two Acts

Music by Adolfe Adam
Scenario by Theophile Gautier based on a theme of Heinrich Heine
Scenery and costumes by James Bailey
Produced by Nicholas Sergeyev after choreography by Coralli

First produced at Covent Garden 12th June, 1946

CAST

GISELLE(a peasant)	*Margot Fonteyn*
COUNT ALBRECHT (disguised as Loys, a villager)	*Alexis Rassine*
BERTHE (Giselle's Mother)	*Elizabeth Kennedy*
HILARION (a woodcutter)	*David Paltenghi*
DUKE OF COURLAND	*David Davenport*
PRINCESS (Daughter of the Duke, betrothed to Albrecht)	*Julia Farron*
WILFRED (Attendant on Albrecht)	*Leslie Edwards*
MYRTHA (Queen of the Wilis)	*Beryl Grey*
ZULME(a Wili)	*Gillian Lynne*
MOYNA (a Wili)	*Gerd Larsen*

COPPELIA

Ballet in Three Acts

Book by Charles Nuitter and Arthur Saint-Leon
Music by Leo Delibes
Scenery and costumes by William Chappell
Choreography by Marius Petipa and Enrico Cecchetti
Reconstructed by Nicholas Sergeyev

First produced at Covent Garden 25th October, 1946

CAST

SWANILDA	Margot Fonteyn
FRANZ	Alexis Rassine
DR. COPPELIUS	Robert Helpmann
COPPELIA	Anne Gieves
BURGOMASTER	David Davenport
HIS WIFE	Patricia Brooks
SWANILDA'S FRIENDS	Pauline Clayden, Anne Negus, June Leighton, Joan Sheldon, Jill Gregory, Elizabeth Kennedy, Avril Navarre, Guinevere Parry
INNKEEPER	Alec Martin
CHINESE DOLL	Veronica Vail
CRUSADER DOLL	Mavis Spence
PIERROT DOLL	Margaret Sear
ASTROLOGER DOLL	Margaret Moffatt
ORIENTAL DOLL	Penelope Asserson
DUKE	Leslie Edwards
DUCHESS	Paula Dunning
FATHER TIME	David Davenport
AURORA	Pauline Clayden
PRAYER	Beryl Grey
HYMEN (Betrothal Dance)	Joan Sheldon, Richard Ellis
WORK	Palma Nye, Gerd Larsen, Lorna Mossford, Rosemary Lindsay

LES SIRÈNES

Music by Lord Berners
Scenery and costumes by Cecil Beaton
Scenario and choreography by Frederick Ashton

First performance Covent Garden 12th November, 1946

CAST

MERMAIDS	Palma Nye, Gilian Lynne
SEAGULLS	Margaret Dale, Alexis Rassine
CHILDREN	Pauline Clayden, Alexander Grant, Guinevere Parry, Mavis Spence
NANNIES	Anne Gieves, Fiorella Keane

GENDARMES	Paul Reymond, Alec Martin
FLOWER WOMAN	Betty Cooper
COUNTESS KITTY	Beryl Grey
CAPTAIN BAY VAVASEUR	Michael Somes
LA BOLERO	Margot Fonteyn
HER CHAUFFEUR	Leslie Edwards
KING HIHAT OF AGPAR	Frederick Ashton
ADELINO CANBERRA (of the Adelaide Opera)	Robert Helpmann

CARNAVAL

Music by Robert Schumann
orchestrated by Gordon Jacob
Scenery and costumes by Bakst
Choreography by Michel Fokine

First produced at Covent Garden 18th November, 1946

CAST

COLUMBINE	Violetta Elvin
CHIARINA	Beryl Grey
ESTRELLA	Julia Farron
PAPILLON	Anne Negus
HARLEQUIN	Harold Turner
PIERROT	Frederick Ashton
EUSEBIUS	Richard Ellis
PANTALON	Paul Reymond
FLORESTAN	Leslie Edwards

LE LAC DES CYGNES

Ballet in Four Acts

Music by Piotr Ilich Tchaikovsky
Scenery and costumes by Leslie Hurry
Choreography by Marius Petipa and Lev Ivanov
Produced by Nicholas Sergeyev

First produced at Covent Garden 19th December, 1946

CAST

PRINCE SIEGFRIED	Robert Helpmann
THE PRINCESS-MOTHER	Jean Bedells
WOLFGANG (Tutor to the Prince)	Paul Reymond
BENNO (The Prince's Friend)	Leslie Edwards
A PEASANT GIRL	June Leighton
ODETTE	Margot Fonteyn
CYGNETS	Avril Navarre, Anne Negus, Pauline Clayden, Violetta Elvin

Two Swans	*Gillian Lynne, Rosemary Lindsay*
Von Rothbart (a wicked Magician)	*David Davenport*
Odile (His Daughter)	*Margot Fonteyn*
Pas de Trois	*Harold Turner, Margaret Dale, Joan Sheldon*
Spanish Dance	*Palma Nye, Julia Farron, Michael Somes, John Hart*
Czardas	*Violetta Elvin, Alexander Grant, June Leighton, Margaret Sear, Jill Gregory, Fiorella Keane, Kenneth Melville, Gaston Lapere, Paul Reymond, Franklin White*
Mazurka	*Gerd Larsen, Richard Ellis, Lorna Mossford, Leslie Edwards, Christine du Boulay, Paddy Stone, Paula Dunning, Norman Thomson*

THE THREE-CORNERED HAT

Ballet by Martinez Sierra after a fable by Alarcon

Music by Manuel de Falla
Scenery and costumes by Picasso
Choreography by Léonide Massine
First produced at Covent Garden 6th February, 1947

CAST

The Miller	*Leonide Massine*
The Miller's Wife	*Margot Fonteyn*
The Governor	*John Hart*
The Governor's Wife	*Paula Dunning*
The Dandy	*Alexander Grant*
Police	*David Davenport, Leslie Edwards, John Field, Stanley Hall, Terence Theobald, Alec Martin*
Fools	*Gilbert Brasler, Gaston Lapere*
Beggars	*Pirnon Aldabalde, Elizabeth Kennedy*
Singer	*Vera Hoddinott*

LA BOUTIQUE FANTASQUE

Ballet in One Act

Music by Gioacchino Rossini
orchestrated by Ottorino Respighi
Curtain, scenery and costumes by André Derain
Choreography by Léonide Massine
First produced at Covent Garden 27th February, 1947

CAST

The Shopkeeper	*John Hart*
His Assistant	*Henry Legerton*
A Thief	*Paul Reymond*
An Old English Maid	*Joy Newton*
Her Friend	*Pat Brooks*
An American	*Leslie Edwards*
His Wife	*Jean Bedells*
Their Son	*Tony Tarver*
Their Daughter	*Margaret Dale*
A Russian Merchant	*David Davenport*
His Wife	*Palma Nye*
Their Son	*Pirmin Aldabalde*
Their Four Daughters	*Joan Sheldon, June Leighton, Guinevere Parry, Veronica Vail*
Two Assistants	*Terence Theobald, Alec Martin*
Two Dolls	*Jill Gregory, Anne Negus*
Tarantella Dancers	*Julia Farron, Harold Turner*
The Queen of Clubs	*June Brae*
The Queen of Hearts	*Pamela May*
The King of Spades	*Paddy Stone*
The King of Diamonds	*Richard Ellis*
The Snob	*Alexis Rassine*
The Melon Hawker	*Franklin White*
A Cossack Girl	*Violetta Elvin*
A Cossack Chief	*Michael Somes*
Five Cossacks	*Kenneth Melville, Norman Thomson, Stanley Hall, John Field, Gaston Lapere*
Dancing Poodles	*Pauline Clayden, Alexander Grant*
Can-Can Dancers	*Moira Shearer, Leonide Massine*

CHECKMATE

Ballet in One Scene with Prologue

Music by Arthur Bliss
Scenery and costumes by E. McKnight Kauffer
Choreography by Ninette de Valois
First produced at Covent Garden 18th November, 1947

CAST

Love } Death } Two Players	*Jean Bedells, Franklin White*
Red Pawns	*Margaret Dale, Avril Navarre, Jill Gregory, Anne Negus, Elizabeth Kennedy, Pauline Clayden, Guinevere Parry, Dorothea Zaymes*
First Red Knight	*Harold Turner*

Second Red Knight	*John Hart*
The Black Knights	*Richard Ellis, John Field*
The Black Queen	*Pamela May*
The Red Queen	*Julia Farron*
The Red King	*Gordon Hamilton*
The Red Bishops	*Paul Reymond, Henry Legerton*
The Red Castles	*Leslie Edwards, Stanley Hall*
Black Pawns	*Gillian Lynne, Rosemary Lindsay, Lorna Mossford, Joan Grantham, Jean Stokes, Christine du Boulay, Palma Nye, Thekla Russell*
The Black Castles	*David Davenport, Alfred Roderigues*

MAM'ZELLE ANGOT

Ballet in Three Scenes by Léonide Massine

Music selected from the works of Alexandre Charles Lecocq orchestrated by Gordon Jacob
Scenery and costumes by André Derain
Choreography by Léonide Massine

First produced at Covent Garden 26th November, 1947

CAST

The Aristocrat	*Moira Shearer*
The Caricaturist	*Michael Somes*
A Government Official	*John Hart*
Mam'zelle Angot	*Margot Fonteyn*
A Barber	*Alexander Grant*
The Chief of Police	*Franklin White*
Two Gendarmes	*Paul Reymond, Ray Powell*
The Butcher	*Leslie Edwards*
The Tailor	*Henry Legerton*
The Bootmaker	*John Field*
The Fishwife	*Margaret Dale*
The Florist	*Jill Gregory*
The Seller of Fruit	*Anne Negus*
The Seller of Vegetables	*Avril Navarre*
Three Ladies	*Jean Bedells, Palma Nye, Thekla Russell*
Two Children	*Guinevere Parry, Veronica Vail*
The Officer	*Richard Ellis*

SCENES DE BALLET

Music by Igor Stravinsky
Scenery and costumes by André Beaurepaire
Choreography by Frederick Ashton

First performance Covent Garden 11th February, 1948

CAST

Margot Fonteyn, Michael Somes, Alexander Grant, John Field, Donald Britton, Philip Chatfield, Avril Navarre, Pauline Clayden, Margaret Dale, Anne Heaton, Gerd Larsen, Gillian Lynne, Rosemary Lindsay, Anne Negus, Lorna Mossford, Jill Gregory, Nadia Nerina, Jean Stokes

JOB

(Being Blake's Vision of the Book of Job)
A Masque for Dancing by Geoffrey Keynes and Gwendolen Raverat

Music by Vaughan Williams
Scenery and costumes designed by John Piper
Choreography by Ninette de Valois

First produced at Covent Garden 20th May, 1948

CAST

Job	*David Davenport*
His Wife	*Jean Bedells*
His Three Daughters	*Julia Farron, Gerd Larsen, Palma Nye*
His Seven Sons	*Alexander Grant, Franklin White, Gilbert Vernon, Henry Legerton, Donald Britton, Tony Tarver, Ray Powell*
Satan	*Robert Helpmann*
War, Pestilence, Famine	*Donald Britton, Alexander Grant, Ray Powell*
The Three Messengers	*John Hart, Michael Somes, John Field*
The Three Comforters	*Franklin White, Henry Legerton, Paul Reymond*
Elihu	*Alexis Rassine*
Job's Spiritual Self	*Alfred Roderigues*

223

CLOCK SYMPHONY

A Fairy Tale in One Act by Léonide Massine

Music by Joseph Haydn
Scenery and costumes by Christian Berard
Choreography by Léonide Massine

First performance Covent Garden 25th June,
1948

CAST

THE CLOCKMAKER	*Alexander Grant*
THE KING	*Leslie Edwards*
THE PRINCESS	*Moira Shearer*
THE PRINCE	*Harold Turner*
HIS PAGE	*Tony Tarver*
THE DUKE	*Donald Britton*
HIS PAGE	*Gilbert Vernon*
THE BIRD	*Anne Negus*
THE LIZARD	*Henry Legerton*
THE MANDARIN	*Franklin White*
HIS WIFE	*Anne Heaton*
GENIE OF THE LIGHTNING	*Michael Somes*
GENIE OF THE RIVER	*Alexis Rassine*
GENIE OF THE MOUNTAIN	*John Hart*
A COMEDIAN	*Ray Powell*
A SAGE	*Paul Reymond*
TWO LADIES-IN-WAITING	*Christine du Boulay,*
	Avril Navarre
PENDULUM	*Ronald Plaisted*
CLOCK HANDS	*Anne Gieves, Veronica Vail*
CHINESE BOY	*Dorothea Zaymes*

❧

DON JUAN

Music by Richard Strauss
Scenery and costumes by Edward Burra
Choreographic impression in One Act by Frederick Ashton

First performance Covent Garden 25th November,
1948

CAST

DON JUAN	*Robert Helpmann*
"LA MORTE AMOUREUSE"	*Margot Fonteyn*
HER ATTENDANTS	*Alfred Rodrigues, Brian Ashbridge*
A YOUNG WIFE	*Moira Shearer*
HER HUSBAND	*Richard Ellis*
AMOURS	*Anne Heaton, Gerd Larsen,*
	Julia Farron, Rosemary Lindsay,
	Nadia Nerina, Gillian Lynne
RIVALS	*John Field, Kenneth Melville,*
	Philip Chatfield

CINDERELLA

Ballet in Three Acts

Devised and produced by Frederick Ashton
Music by Serge Prokofieff
Scenery and costumes by Jean-Denis Malcles
Choreography by Frederick Ashton

First performance Covent Garden 23rd December,
1948

CAST

CINDERELLA	*Moira Shearer*
CINDERELLA'S STEPSISTERS	*Frederick Ashton,*
	Robert Helpmann
CINDERELLA'S FATHER	*Franklin White*
THE RAGGED FAIRY GODMOTHER	*Pamela May*
A TAILOR	*Donald Britton*
DRESSMAKERS	*Anne Negus, Margaret Dale*
THE SHOEMAKER	*Paul Reymond*
THE HAIRDRESSER	*Leslie Edwards*
A JEWELLER	*Henry Legerton*
THE DANCING MASTER	*Harold Turner*
VIOLINISTS	*Kathleen Tierney, Kathleen Sturdy*
THE COACHMAN	*Robert Lunnon*
THE FAIRY SPRING	*Nadia Nerina*
HER PAGES	*Ann Jomeron, Brenda Averty*
THE FAIRY SUMMER	*Violetta Elvin*
HER PAGES	*Annette Page, Jean Cameron*
THE FAIRY AUTUMN	*Pauline Clayden*
HER PAGES	*Karen Bliss, Jean Slater*
THE FAIRY WINTER	*Beryl Grey*
HER PAGES	*Doreen Tempest, Wendy Barker*
THE PRINCE	*Michael Somes*
THE STEPSISTERS' SUITORS	*Alfred Rodrigues,*
	Donald Britton
THE JESTER	*Alexander Grant*
A NEGRO	*Ronald Kaye*

❧

A WEDDING BOUQUET

Words by Gertrude Stein
Music by Lord Berners
Scenery and costumes by Lord Berners
Choreography by Frederick Ashton

First produced at Covent Garden 17th February,
1949

CAST

WEBSTER "Webster was a name that was spoken"	*Palma Nye*
TWO PEASANT GIRLS	*Avril Navarre*
	Sheila Nelson

Two Peasant Boys " They must hurry and get their waggon "   Donald Britton, Brian Shaw

Josephine " She may be wearing a gown newly washed and pressed "   June Brae

Paul " Pleasant, vivacious and quarrelsome "   Harold Turner

John " An elder brother who regrets the illness of his father "   Richard Ellis

Violet " She may be delightful or not, as it happens "   Julia Farron

Ernest " May be a victim of himself "   Ray Powell

Therese " Will be faintly neat "   Gerd Larsen

Julia " Is known as forlorn "   Moira Shearer

Bridegroom " They all speak as if they expected him not to be charming "   Robert Helpmann

Pepe, Julia's dog " Little dogs resemble little girls "   Annette Page

Arthur " Very well I thank you "   Leslie Edwards

Guy " Unknown "   Michael Somes

Four Guests " They incline to oblige only when they stare "   Paula Dunning, Lorna Mossford, Christine du Boulay, Rosemary Lindsay

Two Gendarmes " They make preparations to deal with an exception "   Paul Reymond, Henry Legerton

Bride " Charming! Charming! Charming! "   Margaret Dale

Bridesmaids " They may recognise places "   Anne Negus, Dorothea Zaymes

Orator   Constant Lambert

APPARITIONS

A Ballet on Romantic Themes

Arranged by Constant Lambert to the music of Franz von Liszt
Scenery and costumes by Cecil Beaton
Choreography by Frederick Ashton
First produced at Covent Garden 24th March, 1949

CAST

The Poet   Robert Helpmann
Woman in ball dress   Margot Fonteyn

A Hussar   Harold Turner
A Monk   John Field
Ladies of Fashion   June Brae, Julia Farron, Rosemary Lindsay, Christine du Boulay, Gillian Lynne, Nadia Nerina, Anne Heaton, Dorothea Zaymes
Dandies   Harold Turner, Richard Ellis, Alfred Rodrigues, Philip Chatfield, John Field, Kenneth MacMillan, Kenneth Melville, Gilbert Vernon

FAÇADE

A Ballet freely adapted to music originally written as a setting to poems by Edith Sitwell

Music by William Walton
Scenery and costumes by John Armstrong
Choreography by Frederick Ashton
First produced at Covent Garden 1st August, 1949

CAST

Scotch Rhapsody   April Olrich, Dorothea Zaymes, Gilbert Vernon

Yodelling :
The Milkmaid   Anne Heaton
Mountaineers   Leslie Edwards, Richard Ellis, Philip Chatfield

Polka   Nadia Nerina
Waltz   Gerd Larsen, Christine du Boulay, Paula Dunning, Rosemary Lindsay
Popular Song   Michael Boulton, Donald Britton
Tango :
A Dago   Frederick Ashton
A Debutante   Moira Shearer

DON QUIXOTE

A Ballet in Five Scenes

Scenario and music by Roberto Gerhard
Scenery and costumes by Edward Burra
Choreography by Ninette de Valois
First performance Covent Garden 20th February, 1950

CAST

Don Quixote   Robert Helpmann
Sancho Panza   Alexander Grant
The Housekeeper   Vera Winton

HER NIECE	*June Laverick*
A PRIEST	*Leslie Edwards*
THE BARBER	*Ray Powell*
AN INNKEEPER	*Franklin White*
THE TRAVELLING BARBER	*Harold Turner*
THE LADY DULCINEA	
(Aldonza Lorenzo)	*Margot Fonteyn*
ORIANA	*Christine du Boulay*
ANGELICA	*Gillian Lynne*
URGANDA	*Lorna Mossford*
AMADER OF GAUL	*Philip Chatfield*
ORLANDO FURIOSO	*Kenneth MacMillan*
PALMERIS OF ENGLAND	*Richard Ellis*
SHEPHERD AND SHEPHERDESS	
(The Golden Age)	*Pamela May, Alexis Rassine*
THE LADY BELERMA	*Julia Farron*
DURANDARTE	*Richard Ellis*
MONTESINOS	*John Hart*

☙

BALLET IMPERIAL

Music by Piotr Ilich Tchaikovsky
(Piano Concerto No. 2 in " G " Major)
Scenery and costumes by Eugene Berman
Choreography by George Balanchine
First produced at Covent Garden 5th April,
1950

CAST

Margot Fonteyn, Michael Somes,
Beryl Grey, Nadia Nerina, Pauline Clayden,
John Field, Kenneth MacMillan,
Rowena Jackson, Rosemary Lindsay, Gillian Lynne,
Gerd Larsen, Valerie Taylor, Christine du Boulay,
Lorna Mossford, Julia Farron, Anne Heaton,
Jill Gregory, Dorothea Zaymes, April Olrich,
Avril Navarre, Margaret Dale, Anne Negus,
Margaret Sear, Kenneth Melville, Philip Chatfield,
Gilbert Vernon, Brian Shaw, Richard Ellis,
Bryan Ashbridge

☙

BALLABILE

Ballet by Roland Petit

Music by Chabrier
arranged by Constant Lambert
Scenery and costumes by Antoni Clave
Choreography by Roland Petit
First performance Covent Garden 5th May,
1950

CAST

PRELUDE (BALLABILE)
THE DANCERS PREPARE FOR THE BALLET
A CLASS-ROOM
A SUNDAY ON THE RIVER
A STREET IN THE RAIN
THE CIRCUS ON THE GREEN
IMPRESSIONS OF SPAIN

Violetta Elvin, Alexander Grant,
Anne Negus, Philip Chatfield,
Avril Navarre, Anne Heaton, Margaret Dale,
Kenneth MacMillan, Kenneth Melville, Gilbert Vernon

☙

DAPHNIS AND CHLOÉ

To the music of " Daphnis et Chloe " by Maurice Ravel
Scenery and costumes by John Craxton
Choreography by Frederick Ashton
First performance Covent Garden 5th April,
1951

CAST

CHLOE, A SHEPHERDESS	*Margot Fonteyn*
DAPHNIS, A GOATHERD	*Michael Somes*
LYKANION, A YOUNG MARRIED	
GIRL FROM THE TOWN	*Violetta Elvin*
DORKON, A HERDSMAN	*John Field*
BRYAXIS, a PIRATE CHIEF	*Alexander Grant*
PAN	*Alfred Rodrigues*
NYMPHS OF PAN	*Rosemary Lindsay,*
	Gillian Lynne, Julia Farron

☙

TIRESIAS

A Ballet in Three Scenes by Constant Lambert

Music by Constant Lambert
Scenery and costumes by Isabel Lambert
Choreography by Frederick Ashton
First performance Covent Garden 9th July,
1951

CAST

TIRESIAS (male)	*Michael Somes*
NEOPHYTE	*Margaret Dale*
SNAKES	*Pauline Clayden, Brian Shaw*
TIRESIAS (female)	*Margot Fonteyn*
HER LOVER	*John Field*
ZEUS	*Alfred Rodrigues*
HERA	*Gerd Larsen*

GISELLE

Ballet in Two Acts

Music by Adolphe Adam
Scenario by Theophille Gautier based on a theme by
Heinrich Heine
Scenery and costumes by James Bailey
Produced by Nicholas Sergeyev after choreography by
Coralli

First performance of present production Covent Garden
13th September, 1951

CAST

GISELLE (a peasant girl)	*Moira Shearer*
COUNT ALBRECHT (disguised as Loys, a villager)	*Alexis Rassine*
BERTHE (Giselle's Mother)	*Elizabeth Kennedy*
HILARION (a gamekeeper)	*Leslie Edwards*
THE DUKE OF COURLAND	*Alfred Rodrigues*
THE PRINCESS (the Duke of Courland's daughter)	*Julia Farron*
WILFRED (Count Albrecht's attendant)	*Philip Chatfield*
PAS DE DEUX	*Rowena Jackson, Kenneth MacMillan*
MYRTHA (Queen of the Wilis)	*Beryl Grey*
ZULME (a Wili)	*Julia Farron*
MOYNE (a Wili)	*Rosemary Lindsay*

☙

DONALD OF THE BURTHENS

A Ballet in Two Scenes

Libretto, based on a Scottish legend, by Léonide Massine
Music by Ian Whyte
Scenery and costumes by Robert Colquhoun and Robert
MacBryde
Choreography by Léonide Massine
First performance Covent Garden 12th December,
1951

CAST

DONALD	*Alexander Grant*
DEATH	*Beryl Grey*
THE MOTHER	*Julia Farron*
THREE GOAT MEN	*Ray Powell, Henry Legerton, Franklin White*
THE KING	*Leslie Edwards*
THE KING'S GUEST	*Julia Farron*
COUNTRY DANCE	*Pauline Clayden, Dorothea Zaymes, Anne Heaton, Jill Gregory*

A MIRROR FOR WITCHES

A Ballet in Five Scenes and a Prologue
based on a novel by Esther Forbes

Music by Denis ApIvor
Scenery by Norman Adams
Costumes by Andrée Howard and Norman Adams
Choreography and scenario by Andrée Howard
First performance Covent Garden 4th March,
1952

CAST

A WITCH	*Rosemary Valaire*
DOLL (her daughter as a child)	*Judith Sinclair*
BILBY (a ship's captain)	*Leslie Edwards*
HANNAH (his wife)	*Julia Farron*
DOLL (their foster child as a young girl)	*Anne Heaton*
TITUS (a young man of the village)	*Philip Chatfield*
THE TWINS (his sisters)	*Margaret Dale, Joan Benesh*
THE STRANGER	*John Hart*
PRIESTS	*Franklin White, Gilbert Vernon*

☙

BONNE-BOUCHE

A Cautionary Tale

Music by Arthur Oldham
Scenery and costumes by Osbert Lancaster
Choreography and scenario by John Cranko
First performance Covent Garden 4th April,
1952

CAST

A MOTHER	*Pamela May*
HER DAUGHTER	*Pauline Clayden*
THE LOVER	*Brian Shaw*
A RICH OLD NEIGHBOUR	*John Hart*
HIS BUTLER	*Henry Legerton*
ARTISTIC NEIGHBOURS	*Kenneth MacMillan, Rosemary Valaire*
THEATRICAL NEIGHBOURS	*Kenneth Melville, Julia Farron*
SPORTY NEIGHBOURS	*Philip Chatfield, Rosemary Lindsay*
AN OFFICER	*Gilbert Vernon*
HIS PAST	*Fiorella Keane, June Lesley*
THE LEAGUE OF LIGHT	*Leslie Edwards, Franklin White, Ray Powell, Anne Heaton, Margaret Dale, April Olrich*
A BLACK KING	*Alexander Grant*
HIS CHAMBERLAINS	*John Sale, Douglas Steuart*

HIS WITCH DOCTOR		*Peter Clegg*
HIS CHAUFFEUR		*Colin Worth*
REPORTER		*Franklin White*
TWO POLICEMEN		*Henry Naughton, Ronald Hynd*

✿

SYLVIA

Ballet in Three Acts
Based on Tasso's Aminta

Music by Leo Delibes
Scenery and costumes by Robin and Christopher Ironside
Choreography by Frederick Ashton

First performance Covent Garden 3rd September,
1952

CAST

SYLVIA	*Margot Fonteyn*
AMINTA	*Michael Somes*
ORION	*John Hart*
EROS	*Alexander Grant*
SYLVANS	*Ray Powell, Peter Clegg,*
	Antony Manning, Henry Legerton,
	Franklin White, Douglas Steuart
NAIADS	*Dorothea Zaymes, Anne Heaton,*
	Angela Walton
DRYADS	*Gerd Larsen, April Olrich,*
	Avril Navarre
SLAVES	*Brian Shaw, Peter Clegg*
ORION'S CONCUBINES	*Dorothea Zaymes, Shirley Bateman*
DIANA	*Julia Farron*
GOATS	*Pauline Clayden, Brian Shaw*
APOLLO	*Kenneth Melville*
THE MUSES :	
THE DANCE	*Rosemary Lindsay*
TRAGEDY, COMEDY, HISTORY	*Dorothea Zaymes,*
	Margaret Dale, Gerd Larsen
EPIC POETRY, LYRIC POETRY,	
EROTIC POETRY	*Catherine Boulton,*
	Meriel Evans, Dierdre Dixon
SUBLIME HYMNS,	
ASTRONOMY	*Avril Navarre,*
	Angela Walton
CERES	*Anne Heaton*
JASEION	*Philip Chatfield*
PERSEPHONE	*April Olrich*
PLUTO	*Ray Powell*

LE LAC DES CYGNES

Ballet in Four Acts

Music by Piotr Ilich Tchaikovsky
Scenery and costumes by Leslie Hurry
Choreography by Marius Petipa and Lev Ivanov
Produced by Nicholas Sergeyev
Present production revised by Ninette de Valois
Choreography for the Pas de Six in Act I and the
Neopolitan Dance in Act III by Frederick Ashton
Revised production first performed at Covent Garden

18th December, 1952

CAST

PRINCE SIEGFRIED	*John Field*
THE PRINCESS-MOTHER	*Pamela May*
WOLFGANG (the Prince's Tutor)	*Ray Powell*
BENNO (the Prince's Friend)	*Leslie Edwards*
PAS DE SIX	*Rosemary Lindsay, Mary Drage,*
	Svetlana Beriosova, Alexander Grant,
	Kenneth Melville, Philip Chatfield
PAS DE TROIS	*Brian Shaw, Rowena Jackson,*
	Pauline Clayden
A PEASANT GIRL	*Anne Heaton*
ODETTE (the Swan Princess)	*Beryl Grey*
CYGNETS	*Margaret Dale, Pauline Clayden,*
	Dorothea Zaymes, Angela Walton
FOUR SWANS	*Mary Drage, Svetlana Beriosova,*
	Julia Farron, Greta Hamby
VON ROTHBART (a wicked	
magician)	*Alfred Rodrigues*
ODILE (his daughter)	*Beryl Grey*
MASTER OF CEREMONIES	*Leslie Edwards*
CZARDAS	*Anne Heaton, Ray Powell,*
	Dorothea Zaymes, April Olrich,
	Avril Navarre, Fiorella Keane,
	Peter Clegg, Franklin White,
	Henry Legerton, Douglas Steuart
SPANISH DANCE	*Gerd Larsen, Rosemary Lindsay,*
	Kenneth Melville, Gilbert Vernon
NEOPOLITAN DANCE	*Julia Farron, Alexander Grant*
MAZURKA	*Greta Hamby, Svetlana Beriosova,*
	Rosemary Valaire, Wendy Winn,
	Philip Chatfield, Bryan Ashbridge,
	Ronald Hynd, Desmond Doyle

THE SHADOW

A Ballet in One Scene

Music by Erno von Dohnanyi
Scenery and costumes by John Piper
Choreography and scenario by John Cranko

First performance Covent Garden 3rd March,
1953

CAST

A Youth	*Philip Chatfield*
His Romantic Love	*Svetlana Beriosova*
The Shadow	*Bryan Adhbridge*
A Young Girl	*Rosemary Lindsay*
Her Lovers	*Brian Shaw, Desmond Doyle,*
	Ronald Hynd

VENEZIANA

Music from the Operas of Gaetano Donizetti,
arranged and orchestrated by Denis ApIvor
Scenery and costumes by Sophie Fedorovitch
Choreography by Andrée Howard

First performance Covent Garden 9th April,
1953

CAST

Ladies	*Dorothea Zaymes, Angela Walton,*
	Joan Benesh, Brenda Taylor,
	June Lesley, Fiorella Keane
Cavaliers	*Henry Naughton, Gary Burne,*
	Leon Arnold, Derik Rencher,
	Henry Legerton, Michael Boulton
Masked Ladies	*Meriel Evans, Valerie Adams,*
	Greta Hamby, Rosemary Valaire
Tarantella Dancers	*Anne Heaton, Gerd Larsen,*
	April Olrich, Julia Farron
Young Lovers	*Rosemary Lindsay, Alexander Grant,*
	Wendy Winn, Gilbert Vernon,
	Anya Linden, Douglas Steuart
Punchinello	*Ray Powell*
Harlequins	*Brian Shaw, Peter Clegg*
Columbines	*Pauline Clayden, Rowena Jackson*
La Favorita	*Violetta Elvin*
Gondoliers	*Desmond Doyle, Arnott Mader,*
	Bryan Ashbridge, Philip Chatfield,
	Ronald Hynd

HOMAGE TO THE QUEEN

The Coronation Ballet

Music by Malcolm Arnold
Scenery and costumes by Oliver Messel
Choreography by Frederick Ashton

First performance Covent Garden 2nd June,
1953

CAST

Queen of the Earth	*Nadia Nerina*
Her Consort	*Alexis Rassine*
Her Attendants	*Pauline Clayden, Margaret Dale,*
	Anne Heaton, Michael Boulton,
	Peter Clegg, Ray Powell
Pas de Six	*Joan Benesh, June Lesley,*
	Avril Navarre, April Olrich,
	Angela Walton, Dorothea Zaymes
Queen of the Waters	*Violetta Elvin*
Her Consort	*John Hart*
Her Attendants	*Catherine Boulton, Shirley Bateman,*
	Cynthia Mayan, Deirdre Dixon,
	Brenda Taylor, Anya Linden,
	Fiorella Keane, Yvonne English
Pas de Trois	*Brian Shaw, Julia Farron,*
	Rowena Jackson
Queen of Fire	*Beryl Grey*
Her Consort	*John Field*
Spirit of Fire	*Alexander Grant*
Pas de Quatre	*Svetlana Beriosova, Rosemary Lindsay,*
	Bryan Ashbridge, Philip Chatfield
Queen of the Air	*Margot Fonteyn*
Her Consort	*Michael Somes*
Her Attendants	*Valerie Adams, Mary Drage,*
	Greta Hamby, Valerie Taylor, Wendy Winn,
	Rosemary Valaire, Leon Arnold, Gary Burne,
	Ronald Hynd, Henry Legerton,
	Henry Naughton, Douglas Steuart

COPPELIA

Ballet in Three Acts

Book by Charles Nuitter and Arthur Saint-Leon
Music by Leo Delibes
Scenery and costumes by Osbert Lancaster
Choreography by Lev Ivanov and Enrico Cecchitti
Produced by Nicholas Sergeyev
General production revised by Ninette de Valois
Revised production first performed at Covent Garden
2nd March, 1954

SWANILDA	*Nadia Nerina*
FRANZ	*David Blair*
DR. COPPELIUS	*Frederick Ashton*
COPPELIA	*Elaine Thomas*
THE BURGOMASTER	*Harold Turner*
THE INNKEEPER	*Franklin White*
SWANILDA'S FRIENDS	*Pauline Clayden, April Olrich,*
	Dorothea Zaymes, Angela Walton,
	Margaret Dale, Valerie Taylor
A PEASANT GIRL	*Julia Farron*
CHINESE DOLL	*Judith Sinclair*
SPANISH DOLL	*Deirdre Dixon*
SCOTTISH DOLL	*Cynthia Mayan*
ORIENTAL DOLL	*David Boswell*
CRUSADER DOLL	*Donald Macleary*
DUKE	*Ronald Hynd*
AURORA	*Anya Linden*
PRAYER	*Julia Farron*

❧

THE FIREBIRD

A Ballet in Two Scenes

Music by Igor Stravinsky
Scenery and costumes by N. Gontcharova
Choreography by Michel Fokine
Present production revised by
Serge Grigoriev and Liubov Tchernicheva

First performance Edingurgh Festival 23rd August,
1954

(First London performance Covent Garden 31st August,
1954)

CAST

THE FIREBIRD	*Margot Fonteyn*
IVAN TSAREVITCH	*Michael Somes*
THE BEAUTIFUL TSAREVNA	*Svetlana Beriosova*
THE IMMORTAL KOSTCHEI	*Frederick Ashton*
THE ENCHANTED PRINCESSES	*Valerie Taylor,*
	Catherine Boulton, Deirdre Dixon,
	Brenda Taylor, Cynthia Mayan,
	Angela Walton, Shirley Bateman,
	Dorothea Zaymes, Julia Farron,
	Gerd Larsen, Anya Linden,
	Patricia Thorogood
INDIAN GIRLS	*Mary Drage, Meriel Evans,*
	Anne Stringer, Shirley Camp,
	Jennifer Gay, Margaret Mercier

KOSTCHEI'S WIVES	*Joan Benesh, June Lesley,*
	Judith Sinclair, Hylda Zinkin,
	Pauline Barnes, Veronika Leigey,
	Margaret Wing, Valerie Duke,
	Doreen Eastlake, Valmai Ennor,
	Merle Park, Ann Page
YOUTHS	*Peter Glegg, Ray Powell,*
	Franklin White, Henry Legerton,
	Ronald Plaisted, Douglas Steuart
INDIANS	*Bryan Ashbridge, Desmond Doyle,*
	Gary Burne, Dereck Rencher,
	Donald Barclay, Ronald Plaisted
KIKOMORAS	*Donald Macleary, Bryan Palethorpe.*
	Colin Jones, Oliver Symons
THE BELIBOTCHKI	*Keith Milland, Keith Barker,*
	Christopher Newton, David Boswell
KOSTCHEI'S ATTENDANTS	*Leslie Edwards, Arnott Mader*

❧

RINALDO AND ARMIDA

A dance-drama in One Act

Music by Malcolm Arnold
Scenery and costumes by Peter Rice
Choreography by Frederick Ashton

First performance at Covent Garden 6th January,
1955

CAST

RINALDO (a warrior)	*Michael Somes*
ARMIDA (an enchantress)	*Svetlana Beriosova*
SIBILLA (a sorceress)	*Julia Farron*
GANDOLFO (Rinaldo's companion)	*Ronald Hynd*

❧

VARIATIONS ON A THEME OF PURCELL

Music by Benjamin Britten
Scenery and costumes by Peter Snow
Choreography by Frederick Ashton

First performance at Covent Garden 6th January,
1955

CAST

*Elaine Fifield, Nadia Nerina, Rowena Jackson,
Alexander Grant,
David Blair, Philip Chatfield, Michael Boulton,
Ronald Hynd, Ronald Plaisted, Gary Burne,
Catherine Boulton, Deirdre Dixon, Meriel Evans,
Shirley Camp, Margaret Mercier, Merle Park,
Cynthia Mayan, Brenda Taylor, Valerie Taylor,
Judith Sinclair, Dorothea Zaymes, Angela Walton*

MADAME CHRYSANTHEME

Ballet in One Act and five scenes,
adapted from the book by Pierre Loti

(The action takes place throughout the summer of 1885)
Music by Alan Rawsthorne
Choreography by Frederick Ashton
Scenery and costumes by Isabel Lambert
Lighting by John Sullivan

First performance at Covent Garden on April 1,
1955

CAST

Pierre, a French sailor	*Alexander Grant*
Yves, his brother	*Desmond Doyle*
Mme. Chrysantheme	*Elaine Fifield*
Mme. Renoncule, her mother	*Elizabeth Kennedy*
M. Tres-Propre, her father	*Franklin White*
Mr. Kangarou, a marriage broker	*Ray Powell*
Mlle. Wisteria, a courtesan	*Anne Heaton*
Mlle. Pluie d'Avril, a courtesan	*Pauline Clayden*
Mlle. Purete ⎱ Cousins of	*Merle Park,*
Mlle. Prune ⎰ Chrysantheme	*Angela Walton*
A Dignitary	*Leslie Edwards*
Government Officials	*Henry Legerton, Keith Barker*
Geisha Girls	*June Lesley, Dorothea Zaymes, Margaret Mercier, Doreen Wells*
Mousmes, Chrysantheme's friends	*Brenda Taylor, Valerie Taylor, Meriel Evans, Deirdre Dixon, Cynthia Mayan, Shirley Bateman, Patricia Thorogood, Shirley Camp*
Mouskos, Chrysantheme's friends	*Bryan Ashbridge, Douglas Steuart, Derek Rencher, Peter Clegg, Pirmin Trecu, Gary Burne, Ronald Plaisted, Christopher Newton*
Djinns	*Arnott Mader, Donald Barclay, Keith Milland, John Sales, David Boswell, Peter Brownlee*
Bambou, a Boatman and Rickshaw Boy	*Ray Taylor*
Singer	*Joyce Livingstone*

The Sadler's Wells Theatre Ballet

1946-1955

PROMENADE

Music by Haydn, arranged by Edwin Evans
(Nos. 2-5 orchestrated by Gordon Jacob)
Scenery and costumes by Hugh Stevenson
Choreography by Ninette de Valois

First performed at Sadler's Wells Theatre 8th April, 1946

CAST

THE LEPIDOPTERIST		Claude Newman
1. ENTREE		Diana Field, Sheilah O'Reilly, Audrey Harman, Jane Shore, Fiorella Keane, Josephine Gordon, Nancy McNaught
2. RENDEZVOUS		Joan Harris, George Gerhardt
3. PROMENADE		Sheila Nelson
4. PAS-DE-TROIS		Anne Heaton, Eric Hyrst, Frank Ward
5. DANSE DES PAYSANNES	Sheilah O'Reilly, Diana Field, Donald Britton, Pamela Chrimes, Nancy McNaught, Pauline Wadsworth, Hazel Walker, June Day, Thekla Russell
6. FINALE		Full Company

❧

ASSEMBLY BALL

Music by Georges Bizet (Symphony in C)
Scenery and costumes by Andrée Howard
Choreography by Andrée Howard

First performance at Sadler's Wells Theatre on 8th April, 1946

CAST

MASTER OF CEREMONIES	Leo Kersley
GIRLS IN YELLOW	Anne Heaton, Sheila Nelson
YOUNG GIRLS	Diana Field, Sheilah O'Reilly, Audrey Harman, Jane Shore
THE LADY	June Brae
HER CAVALIERS	George Gerhardt, Eric Hyrst
AN ELDERLY GENTLEMAN	Claude Newman

CASSE-NOISETTE (Act III)

Music by Piotr Ilich Tchaikovsky
Scenery and costumes by Mtislav Dobouzhinsky
Choreography by Lev Ivanov
Produced by Nicholas Sergeyev

First produced at Sadler's Wells Theatre 8th April, 1946

CAST

NUT-CRACKER PRINCE	Norman Thomson
THE SUGAR PLUM FAIRY	Margaret Dale
SIX FAIRIES	Joan Harris, Anne Heaton, Hazel Walker, June Day, Pauline Wadsworth, Thekla Russell
CHOCOLAT : Danse Espagnole	Pamela Chrimes, Michael Hogan
CAFE : Danse Arabe	Nancy McNaught
THE : Danse Chinois	Frank Ward, Michael Boulton
BOUFFON	Donald Britton
DANSE DES MIRLETONS	Sheila Nelson, Diana Field, Sheilah O'Reilly, Jane Shore, Josephine Gordon

❧

LES SYLPHIDES

Music by Frederick Chopin
orchestrated by Gordon Jacob
Scenery by Alexander Benois
Choreography by Michel Fokine

First produced at Sadler's Wells Theatre 22nd April, 1946

CAST

Violetta Elvin, June Brae, Joan Harris, Eric Hyrst,
Anne Seymour, Diana Field, Pamela Chrimes, June Day, Josephine Gordon, Greta Hamby, Audrey Harman, Fiorella Keane, Nancy McNaught, Sheila Nelson, Nadia Nerina, Sheilah O'Reilly, Thekla Russell, Jane Shore, Pauline Wadsworth, Hazel Walker

FAÇADE

A Ballet freely adapted to music originally written as a setting to poems by Edith Sitwell

Music by William Walton
Scenery and costumes by John Armstrong
Choreography by Frederick Ashton

First performed at the Sadler's Wells Theatre
29th April, 1946

CAST

SCOTCH RHAPSODY	Diana Field, Sheilah O'Reilly, Michael Boulton
YODELLING SONG :	
THE MILK MAID	Sheila Nelson
MOUNTAINEERS	Kenneth MacMillan, Peter Darrell, Alan Baker
POLKA	Anne Heaton
WALTZ	Joan Harris, Pamela Chrimes, Pauline Wadsworth, Jane Shore
POPULAR SONG	Donald Britton, Alexander Grant
TANGO :	
A DAGO	Frederick Ashton
A DEBUTANTE	June Brae
TARANTELLA	Full Company

❧

KHADRA

Music from " Belshazzar's Feast " by Sibelius
Scenery and costumes by Honor Frost
Choreography by Celia Franca

First performance at Sadler's Wells Theatre on 27th May, 1946

CAST

KHADRA	Sheilah O'Reilly
THE LOVER	Leo Kersley
HIS LADY	Anne Heaton
THE OLD MAN	Alexander Grant
THE HUSBAND	George Gerhardt
THE WIFE	Thekla Russell
LADY CARDING WOOL	Pamela Chrimes
MUSICIANS	Michael Boulton, Frank Ward
LADIES WITH FLOWERS	Diana Field, Jane Shore, Hazel Walker, Audrey Harman
YOUNG MEN	Alan Baker, Donald Britton, Michael Hogan, Kenneth MacMillan

THE GODS GO A-BEGGING

Music by George Frideric Handel,
arranged by Sir Thomas Beecham
Scenery and costumes by Hugh Stevenson
Choreography by Ninette de Valois

First performed at Sadler's Wells Theatre 10th June, 1946

CAST

A SERVING MAID	Anne Heaton
A SHEPHERD	Leo Kersley
TWO SERVING MAIDS	Diana Field, Sheila Nelson
COURT LADIES	Joan Harris, Pamela Chrimes, June Day, Thekla Russell, Pauline Wadsworth
NOBLEMEN	Alan Carter, Eric Hyrst, Peter Darrell, Michael Hogan, Kenneth MacMillan
BLACK LACKEYS	Josephine Gordon, Greta Hamby, Fiorella Keane, Nadia Nerina, Margaret Dady, Frank Ward
MERCURY	Michael Boulton

❧

THE VAGABONDS

Music by John Ireland
Scenery by Vivienne Kernot
Choreography by Anthony Burke

First performance at Sadler's Wells Theatre
29th October, 1946

CAST

THE VAGABOND GIRL	June Brae
HER LOVER	Alan Carter
THE OTHER MAN	Leo Kersley
HIS WOMAN	Pamela Chrimes
VAGABOND WOMEN	June Day, Greta Hamby, Anne Heaton, Nadia Nerina, Thekla Russell, Pauline Wadsworth
VAGABOND MEN	Alan Baker, Donald Britton, John Cranko, Michael Hogan, Eric Hyrst, Kenneth MacMillan
CHILDREN	Diana Field, Josephine Gordon, Sheila Nelson, Sheilah O'Reilly, Frank Ward

THE CATCH

Music: Rumanian Dances by Bela Bartok
Costumes by Alan Carter
Choreography by Alan Carter

First performance at Sadler's Wells Theatre 29th October,
1946

CAST

THE ELDER BROTHER	*Alan Carter*
HIS GIRL FRIEND	*Joan Harris*
THE YOUNGER BROTHER	*Frank Ward*

MARDI GRAS

Music by Leonard Salzedo
Scenario, costumes and scenery by Hugh Stevenson
Choreography by Andrée Howard

First performance at Sadler's Wells Theatre
26th November, 1946

CAST

THE GIRL	*Anne Heaton*
A BOY	*Donald Britton*
A REVELLER IN WHITE	*Leo Kersley*
A CIRCUS DANCER	*Nadia Nerina*
THREE DANCERS IN BLUE	*Joan Harris, Pamela Chrimes.*
	Paula Wadsworth
A PUGILIST	*John Cranko*
A PRIEST	*Anthony Burke*
ACOLYTES	*Jane Shore, Audrey Harman*
SEXTONS	*David Butterfield, William Martin,*
	Ronald Plaisted

THE HAUNTED BALLROOM

A Ballet in Two Scenes

Written and composed by Geoffrey Toye
Scenery and costumes by Motley
Choreography by Ninette de Valois

First performed at Sadler's Wells Theatre 7th January,
1947

CAST

THE MASTER OF TREGINNIS	*Alan Carter*
YOUNG TREGINNIS	*Frank Ward*
ALICIA	*June Brae*
URSULA	*Joan Harris*
BEATRICE	*Thekla Russell*
THE STRANGER PLAYER	*Leo Kersley*
BUTLER	*Donald Britton*
FOOTMEN	*Michael Boulton, Peter Darrell*

BAILEMOS

Music from " Le Cid " by Massenet
Scenery and costumes by Honor Frost
Choreography by Celia Franca

First performance at Sadler's Wells Theatre 4th February,
1947

CAST

PEASANTS	*Celia Franca, Donald Britton*
	Nadia Moore, Michael Hogan,
	Sheilah O'Reilly, Michael Boulton
NOBLES	*Pauline Wadsworth, Alan Carter,*
	Pamela Chrimes, Anthony Burke,
	Jane Shore, John Cranko

LA FÊTE ETRANGE

Music by Gabriel Faure, orchestrated by Lennox Berkeley
Scenery and costumes by Sophie Fedorovitch
Choreography by Andrée Howard

First performance at Sadler's Wells Theatre 25th March,
1947

CAST

A COUNTRY BOY	*Donald Britton*
THE BRIDE	*June Brae*
THE BRIDEGROOM	*Anthony Burke*
GUESTS	*Anne Heaton, Nadia Moore, Michael Boulton,*
	Jane Shore, Greta Hamby, Pamela Chrimes,
	June Day, Pauline Wadsworth,
	Hazel Walker, Peter Darrell,
	Kenneth MacMillan, John Cranko,
	Sheila Nelson, Diana Field, Josephine Gordon,
	Frank Ward
THE SINGER	*Patricia Hughes*

ADIEU

Music by Scarlatti
Scenery and costumes by Hugh Stevenson
Choreography by John Cranko

First performance at Theatre Royal, Brighton 19th May,
1947

CAST

THE NYMPH	*Jane Shore*
HER LOVER	*David Poole*
A WARRIOR	*Donald Britton*
ATTENDANTS	*Greta Hamby, Hazel Walker*

CARNAVAL

Music by Schumann, orchestrated by Gordon Jacob
Scenery and costumes by Bakst
Choreography by Michel Fokine

First performed at the Theatre Royal, Brighton, 21st May, 1947

CAST

COLUMBINE	*Anne Heaton*
CHIARINA	*Pauline Wadsworth*
ESTRELLA	*Hazel Walker*
PAPILLON	*Nadia Moore*
HARLEQUIN	*Donald Britton*
PIERROT	*Leo Kersley*
EUSEBIUS	*Anthony Burke*
PANTALOON	*Peter Darrell*
FLORESTAN	*Kenneth MacMillan*
VALSE NOBLE	*Pamela Chrimes, Greta Hamby, Jane Shore, Diana Field, John Cranko, David Poole, Michael Boulton, Michael Hogan*
PHILISTINES	*Ruth Clark, Elaine Fifield, Josephine Gordon, Barbara Fewster*

☙

TRITSCH-TRATSCH

Music by Johann Strauss
Costumes by Hedley Briggs
Choreography by John Cranko

First performance at the Sadler's Wells Theatre on 20th September, 1947

CAST

THE GIRL	*Elaine Fifield*
THE SAILORS	*Michael Boulton, David Poole*

☙

VALSES NOBLES ET SENTIMENTALES

Music by Ravel
Scenery and costumes by Sophie Fedorovitch
Choreography by Frederick Ashton

First performance at Sadler's Wells Theatre on 1st October, 1947

CAST

Donald Britton, Anne Heaton, Michael Boulton, Elaine Fifield, Maryon Lane, Jane Shore, Yvonne Barnes, Kenneth MacMillan, Michael Hogan, Peter Darrell

LES RENDEZ-VOUS

Ballet Divertissement

Music by Auber
Scenery and costumes by William Chappell
Choreography by Frederick Ashton

First performed at Sadler's Wells Theatre 26th December, 1947

CAST

ENTREE DES PROMENEURS	*Sheilah O'Reilly, Donald Britton, Ruth Clark, Stella Claire, Stella Farrance, Diana Field Greta Hamby, Jane Shore, Peter Darrell, David Gill, Michael Hogan, David Poole, Pirmin Trecu*
PAS DE QUATRE	*Patricia Miller, Maryon Lane, Irene Surtees, Maureen Bruce*
VARIATION	*Michael Boulton*
ADAGE DES AMOUREUX	*Elaine Fifield, Michael Boulton,*
PAS DE TROIS	*Sheilah O'Reilly, Donald Britton, Pirmin Trecu*
VARIATION	*Elaine Fifield*
PAS DE SIX	*Donald Britton, Peter Darrell, David Gill, Michael Hogan, David Poole, Pirmin Trecu*
SORTIE DES PROMENEURS	

☙

PARURES

Music by Piotr Ilich Tchaikovsky
Scenery and costumes by Vivienne Kernot
Choreography by Anthony Burke

First performance at Sadler's Wells Theatre on 21st January, 1948

CAST

Elaine Fifield, Leo Kersley, Patricia Miller, Michael Boulton, Sheilah O'Reilly, Pirmin Trecu, Diana Field, Irene Surtees, Maryon Lane, David Poole, Pauline Wadsworth, Michael Hogan, Stella Claire, Kenneth MacMillan, Jane Shore, Greta Hamby

CHILDREN'S CORNER

Music by Claude Debussy
Scenery and costumes by Jan le Witt
Choreography by John Cranko

First performance Sadler's Wells Theatre 6th April,
1948

CAST

THE GOLLIWOG	*David Poole*
THE WOODEN DOLL	*Jane Shore*
MADEMOISELLE PIQUANT	*Patricia Miller*
THE GREAT ADMIRER OF MADEMOISELLE PIQUANT	*Kenneth MacMillan*
THE MONKEY OF UKUBABA	*Annette Page*
MERRY-GO-ROUND TINSEL FAIRIES	*Sheilah O'Reilly, Stella Farrance, Maryon Lane*

❧

CAPRIOL SUITE

Music by Peter Warlock
Scenery and costumes by William Chappell
Choreography by Frederick Ashton

First performed at Sadler's Wells Theatre on 5th October,
1948

CAST

BASSE DANSE	*Maureen Bruce, Stella Farrance, Michael Boulton, Pirmin Trecu*
PAVANE	*Jane Shore, David Poole, Hans Zullig*
TORDION	*Patricia Miller, Michael Boulton*
PIEDS EN L'AIR	*Jane Shore, Stella Claire, David Poole, Hans Zullig*
MATTACHINS	*Michael Boulton, David Blair, David Gill, Pirmin Trecu*

❧

SELINA

A Ballet by Andrée Howard and Peter Willams

Music by Rossini, arranged by Guy Warrack
Scenery by Peter Williams
Choreography and costumes by Andrée Howard

First performance Sadler's Wells Theatre 16th November,
1948

CAST

SIMPLICE (a Poet)	*Hans Zullig*
SELINA (a Girl)	*Elaine Fifield*
TOM (her Brother)	*Pirmin Trecu*
LORD RAVENSGARTH (her Stepfather)	*David Gill*
AGNES (a Witch)	*Stanley Holden*
NAILA (the Chief Naiad)	*Stella Claire*
NAIADS	*Patricia Miller, Joan Cadzow, Mary Drage, Stella Farrance, Greta Hamby, Maryon Lane, Sheilah O'Reilly, Jane Shore, Veronica Vail, Elizabeth Christie*

❧

ÉTUDE

A Choreographic Study

Music by Anthony Hopkins
Scenery and costumes by Vivienne Kernot
Choreography by Nancy McNaught

First performance Sadler's Wells Theatre 15th March,
1949

CAST

FIRST MOVEMENT : *David Poole, Sheilah O'Reilly, Hans Zullig, Maryon Lane, Maureen Bruce, Jane Shore, Stella Claire, Stella Farrance, Barbara Fewster, Mary Drage, Joan Cadzow, David Gill, David Blair, Michael Hogan, Peter Wright, Pirmin Trecu*

SECOND MOVEMENT :

PAS DE SIX	*Jane Shore, Stella Claire, Stella Farrance, Pirmin Trecu, Michael Hogan, Peter Wright*
PAS SEUL	*Sheilah O'Reilly*
PAS DE QUATRE	*Maryon Lane, Maureen Bruce, David Gill, David Blair*

THIRD MOVEMENT : *David Poole, Sheilah O'Reilly, Hans Zullig and ensemble*

❧

BEAUTY AND THE BEAST

Music by Ravel
Scenery and costumes by Margaret Kaye
Choreography by John Cranko

First performance Sadler's Wells Theatre 20th December,
1949

CAST

BEAUTY	*Patricia Miller*
THE BEAST	*David Poole*

LE LAC DES CYGNES (Act II)

Music by Piotr Ilich Tchaikovsky
Scenery and costumes by Hugh Stevenson
Choreography by Marius Petipa and Lev Ivanov
Produced by Nicholas Sergeyev

First produced at the Embassy Theatre, Peterborough,
23rd May, 1949

CAST

ODETTE (the Swan Queen)	*Elaine Fifield*
PRINCE SIEGFRIED	*David Poole*
BENNO (the Prince's Friend)	*Hans Zullig*
CYGNETS	*Phyllis Kennedy, Maryon Lane, Patricia Miller, Veronica Vail*
TWO SWANS	*Joan Cadzow, Mary Drage*
SWANS	*Maureen Bruce, Elizabeth Christie, Stella Farrance, Sheilah O'Reilly, Pauline Harrop, Karen Bliss, Noreen Sopwith, Maureen Swanson*
HUNTSMEN	*David Blair, David Gill, Maurice Metliss, Peter Wright*

❧

SEA CHANGE

Music by Sibelius
Scenery and costumes by John Piper
Choreography by John Cranko

First performance Gaiety Theatre, Dublin, 18th July,
1949

CAST

THE SKIPPER	*David Poole*
HIS WIFE	*Joan Cadzow*
THEIR CHILD	*Maureen Swanson*
THE OLD WOMAN	*Jane Shore*
HER SON	*David Blair*
A FISHERMAN	*Michael Hogan*
HIS YOUNG WIFE	*Sheilah O'Reilly*
THE PASTOR	*Hans Zullig*

EL DESTINO

Music by Manuel Lazareno
Costumes by Hugh Stevenson
Choreography by Angelo Andes

First performance Sadler's Wells Theatre 31st January,
1950

CAST

THE FORTUNE-TELLER	*Kathleen Gorham*
SEVILLANAS	*Stella Claire, Sheilah O'Reilly, Jane Shore, Stella Farrance, Phyllis Kennedy, Pirmin Trecu, Peter Wright, David Blair, David Gill, Stanley Holden*
ZAPATEADO	*Pirmin Trecu*
DUO	*Sheilah O'Reilly, Pirmin Trecu*
JOTA ARAGONESA	*Maryon Lane, Pirmin Trecu, Patricia Miller, Maureen Bruce, Joan Cadzow, Mary Drage, Peter Wright, David Blair, Donald McAlpine, Maurice Metliss*

❧

SUMMER INTERLUDE

Music from " Old Airs and Dances," arranged by Respighi
Scenery and costumes by Sophie Fedorovitch
Choreography by Michael Somes

First performance Sadler's Wells Theatre 28th March,
1950

CAST

A VILLAGE GIRL	*Patricia Miller*
A VILLAGE BOY	*Pirmin Trecu*
BATHERS	*Elaine Fifield, David Blair, Joan Cadzow, Jane Shore, Michael Hogan, Maureen Swanson, Veronica Vail, Sheilah O'Reilly, Stanley Holden, Donald McAlpine, Maureen Bruce, Peter Wright, Stella Claire, David Gill*

❧

TRUMPET CONCERTO

Music by Haydn
Scenery and costumes by Vivienne Kernot
Choreography by George Balanchine

First performance at the Opera House, Manchester,
14th September, 1950

CAST

Svetlana Beriosova, David Blair,
Elaine Fifield, Pirmin Trecu,
David Poole, Maryon Lane,
Shirley Bishop, Maureen Bruce, Joan Cadzow,
Stella Claire, Stella Farrance, Kathleen Gorham,
Sheilah O'Reilly, Veronica Vail

❧

PASTORALE

Music: Divertimento No. 2 in D, K. 131 by Mozart
Scenery and costumes by Hugh Stevenson
Choreography by John Cranko
First performance Sadler's Wells Theatre 19th December,
1950

CAST

PHILLIDA	Patricia Miller
CORYDON	Pirmin Trecu
LAMILIA	Svetlana Beriosova
MELANTHUS	David Poole
DAMON	David Blair
DIAPHENIA	Elaine Fifield
PARAMOURS	Maureen Bruce, Pauline Harrop, Peter Wright, Michael Hogan

❧

THE PROSPECT BEFORE US

A Ballet in Seven Scenes

Music by William Boyce arranged by Constant Lambert
Scenery and costumes by Roger Furse
(after Thomas Rowlandson)
Choreography and scenario by Ninette de Valois
First performed at Sadler's Wells Theatre on
13th February, 1951

CAST

MR. TAYLOR (Manager of the King's Theatre)	David Poole
MR. O'REILLY (Manager of the Pantheon)	Robert Helpmann
MONSIEUR NOVERRE (Choreographer and Ballet Dancer)	David Gill
MADAME NOVERRE	Barbara Fewster
MADEMOISELLE THEODORE (Premiere Danseuse)	Elaine Fifield
MONSIEUR DIDELOT	David Blair
MONSIEUR VESTRIS	Pirmin Trecu
PATRONS OF THE BALLET	Joan Cadzow, Maurice Metliss

TWO DANCERS	Maryon Lane, Sheila O'Reilly
A DANCER	Svetlana Beriosova
CUPID	Patricia Miller
THREE LAWYERS	Don Gillies, Michael Hogan, Peter Wright

❧

PINEAPPLE POLL

A Ballet freely adapted from the Bab Ballad
"The Bumboat Woman's Story" by W. S. Gilbert

Music by Arthur Sullivan,
arranged by Charles Mackerras
Scenery and costumes by Osbert Lancaster
Choreography by John Cranko
First performance at Sadler's Wells Theatre 13th March,
1951

CAST

PINEAPPLE POLL (a Bumboat Woman)	Elaine Fifield
JASPER (Pot Boy at "The Steam Packet")	David Poole
CAPTAIN BELAYE (of H.M.S. Hot Cross Bun)	David Blair
BLANCHE (his Fiancée)	Stella Claire
MRS. DIMPLE (her Aunt)	Sheilah O'Reilly
THE CREW (of H.M.S. Hot Cross Bun)	David Gill, Michael Hogan Stanley Holden, Donald McAlpine, Maurice Metliss, Peter Wright
SWEETHEARTS, WIVES, etc.	Yvonne Barnes, Shirley Bishop, Joan Cadzow, Stella Farrance, Maryon Lane, Doreen Tempest

❧

HARLEQUIN IN APRIL

Music by Richard Arnell
Scenery and costumes by John Piper
Choreography by John Cranko
First performance at Sadler's Wells Theatre on 8th May,
1951

CAST

PIERROT'S SONG	Stanley Holden
HARLEQUIN	David Blair
PLANTS	Patricia Miller, Maureen Bruce, Stella Farrance, Pauline Harrop, Maryon Lane, David Gill, Don Gillies, Pirmin Trecu

COLUMBINE	*Patricia Miller*
THE UNICORN	*Maurice Metliss, David Poole*
MAGICAL DUPLICATIONS	
OF THE UNICORN	
	Don Gillies, David Gill,
	Donald McAlpine, Pirmin Trecu,
	Peter Wright, Shirley Bishop,
	Joan Cadzow, Sara Neil

ℬ

THE RAKE'S PROGRESS

A Ballet by Gavin Gordon after William Hogarth

Music by Gavin Gordon
Scenery and costumes by Rex Whistler after William
Hogarth
Choreography by Ninette de Valois
First performed at Sadler's Wells Theatre 18th June,
1952

CAST

THE RAKE	*Alexander Grant*
THE TAILOR	*David Poole*
THE JOCKEY	*Walter Trevor*
THE FENCING MASTER	*Kenneth MacMillan*
THE BRAVO	*Maurice Metliss*
THE HORN BLOWER	*Donald McAlpine*
THE DANCING MASTER	*Donald Britton*
THE BETRAYED GIRL	*Sheila O'Reilly*
HER MOTHER	*Veronica Vail*
LADIES OF THE TOWN	*Pauline Wadsworth,*
	Romayne Austin, Doreen Tempest,
	Shirley Bishop, Stella Farrance
THE DANCER	*Stella Claire*
THE SERVANT	*Joan Blakeney*
THE RAKE'S FRIEND	*David Gill*
THE BALLAD SINGER	*Hermione Harvey*
MUSICIANS	*Arnott Mader, Donald McAlpine*
THE CREDITORS	*Kenneth MacMillan, Maurice Metliss,*
	David Poole
THE GAMBLERS	*Walter Trevor, Donald McAlpine,*
	Maurice Metliss
THE GENTLEMAN	
WITH A ROPE	*Stanley Holden*
THE CARD PLAYER	*David Gill*
THE VIOLINIST	*Kenneth MacMillan*
THE SAILOR	*David Poole*
THE KING	*Graham McCormack*
THE POPE	*Arnott Mader*
VISITORS	*Romayne Austin, Shirley Bishop,*
	Stella Farrance

REFLECTION

Music by John Gardner
Scenery and costumes by Keith New
Scenario and choreography by John Cranko
First performance at the Empire Theatre, Edinburgh,
during the Edinburgh Festival, 21st August, 1952

CAST

NARCISSUS	*David Poole*
ECHO	*Elaine Fifield*
THE LOVERS	*Patricia Miller, Pirmin Trecu*
THE TENDER CHILD	*Sheilah O'Reilly*
THE AGGRESSIVE CHILD	*Donald Britton*
THE ADOLESCENTS	*Yvonne Cartier, Pauline Harrop,*
	Maureen Bruce, Sara Neil,
	Annette Page, David Gill,
	Donald McAlpine, Maurice Metliss,
	David Shields, Walter Trevor

ℬ

COPPELIA

A Ballet in Three Acts

Music by Leo Delibes; third Act orchestrated by
Gordon Jacob
Book by Charles Nuitter and Arthur Saint-Leon
Scenery and costumes by Loudon Sainthill
Choreography by Lev Ivanov and Enrico Cecchetti,
reproduced by Nicholas Sergeyev
First produced at Sadler's Wells Theatre on
4th September, 1951

CAST

SWANILDA	*Elaine Fifield*
FRANTZ	*David Blair*
DR. COPPELIUS	*David Poole*
COPPELIA	*Carlu Carter*
THE BURGOMASTER	*Robert Lunnon*
HIS WIFE	*Hermione Harvey*
SWANILDA'S FRIENDS	*Maureen Bruce, Stella Farrance,*
	Sara Neil, Annette Page,
	Doreen Tempest, Veronica Vail
THE CHINESE DOLL	*Walter Trevor*
THE CRUSADER	*Don Gillies*
THE PIERROT	*Karen Bliss*
THE ASTROLOGER	*Graham McCormack*
THE ORIENTAL DOLL	*Romayne Austin*
DAWN	*Patricia Miller*

PRAYER	*Svetlana Beriosova*
HYMEN (the betrothal dance)	*Sheilah O'Reilly, Donald Britton*
PAS DE DEUX	*Elaine Fifield, David Blair*
DANCE OF THE HARVESTERS	*Yvonne Barnes, Shirley Bishop, Joanne Nisbet, Pauline Wadsworth*
THE DUKE	*Robert Lunnon*
DANCE OF THE HOURS	*Brenda Averty, Romayne Austin, Shirley Bishop, Karen Bliss, Yvonne Barnes, Carlu Carter, Josephine Gordon, Hermione Harvey, Sara Neil, Joanne Nisbet, Annette Page, Margaret Sear*

❧

CASSE-NOISETTE

Music by Piotr Ilich Tchaikovsky
Scenery and costumes by Cecil Beaton
Choreography by Lev Ivanov, revised by Frederick Ashton

First performance of a new production at Sadler's Wells Theatre on 11th September,

1951

CAST

THE QUEEN	*Svetlana Beriosova*
THE KING	*Robert Lunnon*
THE SUGAR PLUM FAIRY	*Elaine Fifield*
THE NUTCRACKER PRINCE	*David Blair*
SUGAR-STICKS	*Patricia Miller, Carlu Carter, Stella Farrance, Annette Page, Veronica Vail*
CHOCOLATE FROM SPAIN	*Sheilah O'Reilly, Margaret Sear, Pirmin Trecu*
COFFEE FROM ARABIA	*Stella Claire, Arnott Mader, Graham McCormack, Peter Wright*
TEA FROM CHINA	*David Gill, Maurice Metliss*
NOUGAT FROM RUSSIA	*Donald Britton, Stanley Holden, Donald McAlpine, Walter Trevor*
CRYSTALLISED FLOWERS	*Maryon Lane, Yvonne Barnes, Maureen Bruce, Josephine Gordon, Sheila Nelson, Sara Neil, Joanne Nisbet, Hermione Harvey, Pauline Wadsworth*

ILE DES SIRÈNES

Music by Claude Debussy
Scenery and costumes by Loudon Sainthill
Choreography by Alfred Rodrigues

First performance at the Sadler's Wells Theatre on 19th September, 1952

CAST

THE MARINER (Palinurus)	*David Blair*
SIRENS	*Elaine Fifield, Maureen Bruce, Margaret Hill, Sara Neil, Annette Page, Doreen Tempest, Pauline Wadsworth*

❧

THE GREAT DETECTIVE

A Ballet after Sir A. Conan Doyle

Music by Richard Arnell
Scenery and costumes by Brian Robb
Choreography by Margaret Dale

First performance at the Sadler's Wells Theatre on 21st January, 1953

CAST

THE GREAT DETECTIVE	*Kenneth MacMillan*
HIS FRIEND, THE DOCTOR	*Stanley Holden*
THE INNOCENT SUSPECT	*David Blair*
THE INFAMOUS PROFESSOR	*Kenneth MacMillan*

❧

BLOOD WEDDING

A Ballet in One Act

Scenery and costumes by Isabel Lambert
Scenario by Denis ApIvor and Alfred Rodrigues, based on the play " Bodas de Sangre " by F. Garcia Lorca
Music by Denis ApIvor
Choreography by Alfred Rodrigues

First performance at Sadler's Wells Theatre 5th June,

1953

CAST

LEONARDO (a married man)	*David Poole*
THE BRIDE	*Elaine Fifield*
THE MOON	*Kenneth MacMillan*
DEATH	*Sheilah O'Reilly*
SERVANT	*Yvonne Cartier*
LEONARDO'S WIFE	*Doreen Tempest*
THE BRIDEGROOM	*Pirmin Trecu*

HIS MOTHER	*Margaret Hill*
THE BRIDE'S FATHER	*Graham McCormack*
THE BRIDE'S FRIENDS	*Sara Neil, Sonya Hana*
THE BRIDEGROOM'S FRIENDS	*David Gill,*
	Maurice Metliss

☙

CARTE BLANCHE

Music by John Addison
Scenery and costumes by Kenneth Rowell
Choreography (dedicated to the memory of Lilian Baylis)
by Walter Gore

First performance at the Empire Theatre, Edinburgh,
during the Edinburgh Festival on 10th September,
1953

CAST

PRELUDE	*Johaar Mosaval and Full Company*
WALTZ	*Yvonne Cartier, Stella Farrance,*
	Doreen Tempest, Pauline Wadsworth,
	Donald Britton, David Gill,
	Stanley Holden, Pirmin Trecu
BAGATELLE	*Margaret Hill, Sheilah O'Reilly,*
	Joanne Nisbet, Maurice Metliss
SCHERZO	*David Shields, Peter Wright*
CASSATION:	
RING MASTER	*David Poole*
TIGHT ROPE WALKER	*Pirmin Trecu*
TRAPEZE ARTISTS	*Sheilah O'Reilly, Donald Britton*
EQUESTRIENNE	*Margaret Hill*
PONY	*Joanne Nisbet, Maurice Metliss*
CLOWNS	*Anette Page, Veronica Vail,*
	Madeleine White, David Shields,
	Peter Wright
INTERLUDE	*Stanley Holden*
ROMANZA	*Margaret Hill, David Poole*

☙

PUERTA DE TIERRA

Bolero

Music by Albeniz
orchestrated by Salabert
Costume designed by Anthony Boyes
Choreography by Roberto Ximenez

First performance at the Sadler's Well Theatre on
11th December, 1953

DANCED BY
Pirmin Trecu

THE LADY AND THE FOOL

Music by Verdi, arranged by Charles Mackerras
Settings and costumes by Richard Beer
Scenario and choreography by John Cranko

First performance at the New Theatre, Oxford, on
25th February, 1954

CAST

MOONDOG	} two clowns	*Kenneth MacMillan*
BOOTFACE		*Johaar Mosaval*
LA CAPRICCIOSA (a beauty)		*Patricia Miller*
SIGNOR MIDAS		*David Gill*
CAPITANO ADONCINO	} her suitors	*Peter Wright*
THE PRINCE OF ARRAGONCA		*David Poole*
SIGNORA SCINTILLARDA (a society hostess)		*Doreen Tempest*
HER LOVERS		*Donald Britton, Pirmin Trecu*
THEIR WIVES		*Sheilah O'Reilly, Sara Neil*

☙

CAFÉ DES SPORTS

Music by Antony Hopkins
Scenery and costumes by Jack Taylor
Choreography by Alfred Rodrigues

First performed by Sadler's Wells Theatre Ballet at
His Majesty's Theatre, Johannesburg, on 24th May,
1954

CAST

URCHIN	*Maryon Lane*
MADAME FLORA, PROPRIETRESS OF THE CAFE	*Margaret Hill*
WAITER	*Gilbert Vernon*
BOURGEOIS COUPLES	*Pauline Wadsworth,*
	Stella Farrance, David Gill,
	Maurice Metliss
THE HEDONIST ARTISTS	*Maureen Bruce, Donald Britton,*
	Pirmin Trecu, and Dorinda Brown,
	Yvonne English, Margaret Lee,
	Valerie Reece
THE ESSENTIALIST ARTISTS:	
PAS DE TROIS	*Doreen Tempest, Sara Neil,*
	Kenneth MacMillan
PAS DE DEUX	*Annette Page, David Poole,*
CYCLISTS	*Stanley Holden, Patrick Hurde,*
	David Shields, Walter Trevor,
	Miro Zolan

DANSES CONCERTANTES

Music by Igor Stravinsky
Choreography by Kenneth MacMillan
Scenery and costumes by Nicholas Georgiadis

First performed by Sadler's Wells Theatre Ballet at
Sadler's Wells Theatre on Tuesday, 18th January,
1955

CAST

Maryon Lane,
Donald Britton, David Poole,
Sara Neil, Gilbert Vernon, Annette Page,
Donald MacLeary, Bryan Lawrence,
Pauline Barnes, Shirley Bishop, Brenda Bolton,
Yvonne English, Yvonne Lakier, Margaret Lee

☙

LES PATINEURS

Music by Giacomo Meyerbeer
arranged by Constant Lambert
Scenery and costumes by William Chappell
Choreography by Frederick Ashton

First performed at Sadler's Wells Theatre on
Saturday, 23rd April, 1955

CAST

ENTREE	*Sara Neil, Doreen Tempest,*
PAS DE HUIT	*Susan Alexander, Joan Blakeney,*
	Diane Forhan, Valerie Reece,
	Bryan Lawrence, Donald MacLeary,
	David Shields, Walter Trevor
VARIATION	*Donald Britton*
PAS DE DEUX	*Annette Page, David Poole*
ENSEMBLE	*Sara Neil, Doreen Tempest,*
	Donald Britton and Pas de Huit
PAS DE TROIS	*Sara Neil, Doreen Tempest,*
	Donald Britton
PAS DE PATINEUSES	*Shirley Bishop, Yvonne English*
ENSEMBLE	*Shirley Bishop, Yvonne English,*
	Bryan Lawrence, Donald MacLeary,
	David Shields, Leslie White
FINALE	*Ensemble*

INDEX

All Ballets are to be found under the heading BALLETS AND DIVERTISSEMENTS
All references to photographs are in bold type

Acoustics, 119, 120
Albert Hall, London, 16
Alhambra Theatre, London, 22, 23, 26, 27, 33, 57, 87
Antonio, 24
Appleyard, Beatrice, in *The Jar*, **41**; in *The Haunted Ballroom*, **43**; in *Barabau*, **45**; in *Façade*, **51**
Argyle, Pearl, **34, 47** (Memorial Library), **70**; in *Mermaid*, 33; in *Lady of Shalott*, 33; in *Bar—aux Folies Bergères*, 33; in *The Gods Go A-Begging*, **46**; in *Pomona*, **48**
Armstrong, John, 50, 135, 145
Ashbridge, Brian, in *The Shadow*, **100**;
Ashton, Frederick, 33, 34, 40, 48, 53, 57, 58, 74, **86**, 87, 88, 89, 90, 118, **127**, 135, 137; in *Façade*, **50, 52, 166**; in *The Firebird*, **94**; in *Les Sirènes*, **164**; in *Nocturne*, **164**; in *Coppelia*, **165**
Astafieva, Seraphine, 58
Auber, 118
Auric, 25, 28
Auriol, M. Vincent, 73, 74

Bach, 118
Bailey, James, 138
Bakst, Léon, 15-20, 23, 24, 26, **27**, 28, 133, 137
Balakirev, 22, 31
Balanchine, George, 28, 29, 58, 88, 89, **176, 179**
Ballet: English style, 33, 56, 63, 88, 90, 158; French, Danish and Italian Schools, 56; 90; in America, 58, 63, 90, 159, 160; Some problems, 158-60; classical tradition, 158, 159; in Europe, 159, 160; modern, 159, 160
Ballet Russe (*see* Russian Ballet)

BALLETS AND DIVERTISSEMENTS
Adam Zero, 89
Amour Vainqueur, L', 134
Apparitions, **53**, 87, **116**, 118, **169**; Décor and costumes, **144**
Après-midi d'un Faune, l', 15, 133
Assembly Ball, **75**, 89
Aurora's Wedding, 27, 57
Baiser de la Fée, 118

Ballabile, **97**, 138, **192**
Ballet Imperial, **98, 179**
Bar—aux Folies Bergères, 33
Barabau, **45**; décor and costumes, **148**
Barber of Seville, 23
Beau Danube, 88
Belle au Bois Dormant, La, 14, 20, 26-8, 30
Biches, Les, 28
Blood Wedding, **79**
Blue Bird, The, **189**
Bonne Bouche, **102**; décor, 138, **157**
Boris Godounov, 15
Boutique Fantasque, La, 22-4, 88, 134, 135, 137

Carnaval, 15, **18**, 19, 20, 118, 133
Casse-Noisette, 14, **38**, 74, **86**, 118
Checkmate, 118, 136
Children's Tales, 20
Choreartium, 88
Chout, 25
Cinderella, **110, 111, 181**
Cléopatre, 19
Comus, 118, 137, **174**
Coppelia, 31, **42**, 74, **83, 84**, 118, **165, 200**; décor, **155**
Coq d'Or, Le, 15, 18
Cotillon, 88, 89
Création du Monde, **43**, 118
Cuadro Flamenco, 28

Dante Sonata, **115**, 118, **182**; décor and costumes, **152**
Daphnis and Chloé, 15, 89, **108**, 138, **194, 197**
Dieu Bleu, Le, 15
Don Quixote, **97**; drop curtain, **149**
Donald of the Burthens, **103**
Douanes, **39, 41**

Enchanted Princess, 20

Façade, **50-2**, 89, 118, 135; décor and costumes, **145**
Facheux, Les, 28, 134
Firebird, **91-6** (*see also* L'Oiseau de Feu)

Giselle, **33**, 74, **104-07**, 118, 122, **163, 199**

Gods Go A-Begging, The, **38, 46, 48**
Good-Humoured Ladies, The, 18, 20

Hamlet, 118, 137
Harlequin in April, **78,** 89
Haunted Ballroom, The **43, 81,** 118
Homage à la Reine, décor and costumes, **153**
Horoscope, 118

Jackdaw and the Pigeons, The, **37**
Jar, The, **41**
Job, 38, 57, 87, 118, **128, 175**

Khadra, **76**

Lac des Cygnes, Le, 118; décor, **150, 151** (see also Swan Lake)
Lady of Shalott, The, 33
Légende de Joseph, La, 15

Marriage of Figaro, 32
Matelots, Les, 28, 88
Mermaid, The, 33
Midnight Sun, The, 20
Miracle in the Gorbals, The, 89, 135, **174;** décor and costumes, **148**
Mirror for Witches, **99**

Narcisse, 15
Nocturne, 87, 118, **164**

Oiseau de Feu, l', 14, 15, 22 (see also The Firebird)

Panorama, 28
Parade, 25
Patineurs, Les, **49,** 118, **193**
Pavillon d'Armide, 136
Petrouchka, 15, 22
Pineapple Poll, **82;** décor, **156**
Pomona, **48,** 117
Présages, 88
Pride, **37**
Prince Igor, 15, 16, 19
Prodigal Son, The, 134
Prospect Before Us, The, 87, 89, **173**
Pulcinella, 25

Quest, The, décor, **146**
Rake's Progress, The, **44, 80,** 87, 118, 136, **136;** décor and costumes, **139-41**
Reflection, **196**
Rendezvous, Les, **40,** 118
Rio Grande, 45, 117
Rossignol, Le, 25, 134

Sacre du Printemps, Le, 15, 20, 25
Sadko, 20
Schéhérazade, 15, 16, **17,** 20, 21, 27, 28, 30, 31
Sea Change, **77,** 136

Shadow, The, **100, 198**
Sirènes, Les, **164, 168**
Sleeping Beauty, The, **29,** 74, 87, 118, 137, **170, 172, 174**
Sleeping Princess, The, **54,** 57 (see also La Belle au Bois Dormant)
Spectre de la Rose, Le, 14, **132**
Swan Lake, 57, 74, 89, 137, **180, 183, 186, 190** (see also Lac des Cygnes)
Sylphides, Les, 20, 56, 89, 118
Sylvia, 31, **112, 113,** 118, 137, **171, 188, 200;** décor and costumes, **154**
Symphonic Variations, 74, 89, 90, 118

Thamar, 22
Tiresias, 89, **101, 170**
Tricorne, Le, 22, 24, 88, 134, 137
Triumph of Neptune, The, 29, 31

Wanderer, The, 118; décor and costumes, 135, **147**
Wedding Bouquet, The, **53, 114,** 118, **174;** décor and costumes, **143**
Wise and Foolish Virgins, The, 118, décor, **142**

Bamford, Freda, in The Haunted Ballroom, **43**
Barbier, George, 16
Barcelona, 17
Barnes, Yvonne, in The Haunted Ballroom, **81**
Baronova, 32, in Beau Danube, 88; in Présages, 88
Baylis, Lilian, 59, 74
Beardsley, Aubrey, 30
Beaton, Cecil, **86,** 144
Beauchamp, Pierre, 58
Beauchant, 134
Beaumont, Mr. Cyril W., 15, 17, 23
Beecham, Sir Thomas, 16, 18
Beethoven, 33, 118
Benois, Nadia, 74, 133, 136
Bérain, 55, 133
Bérard, Christian, 137
Beriosova, Svetlana, 90, **195;** in Assembly Ball, **75;** in The Firebird, **92, 96;** in The Shadow, **100**
Berlioz, 33
Berners, Lord, 28, 31, 53, 118, **127,** 143
Bibiena, 26, 27, 133
Bizet, 31
Blair, David, in Assembly Ball, **75;** in Harlequin in April, **78;** in The Rake's Progress, **80;** in Pineapple Poll, **82;** in Coppelia, **200**
Blasis, Carlo, 58
Bliss, Sir Arthur, 118, **129**
Botticelli, 46
Boucher, 46, 55
Bournonville, 58
Brae, June, in Façade, **51**
Brahms, 33, 118
Braque, 134

Braun, Molly, in *Façade*, **50**
Brianza, Carlotta, in *La Belle au Bois Dormant*, 26
Bull, John, 31
Burne-Jones, 32
Burra, Edward, **45,** 135, 148, 149
Byron, Robert, 26

Cadzow, Joan, in *The Haunted Ballroom*, **81**
Carmargo, 58
Carmargo Society, 33, 118
Cambridge, Festival Theatre, 57
Cassandre, 33
Cecchetti, Enrico, 55, 58; in *La Boutique Fantasque*, 24; in *La Belle au Bois Dormant*, 26
Cecchetti, Josephine, in *The Good-Humoured Ladies*, 19
Chabrier, 28, 31, 118
Chaliapin, 15
Chamberlain, George, 60
Chappell, William, 37-54, 135; in *Job*, 38; in *Création du Monde*, 43; in *Barabau*, **45;** in *The Gods Go A-Begging*, **46;** in *Apparitions*, 53; in *The Wedding Bouquet*, 53
Chatfield, Philip, in *The Shadow*, **100;** in *Sylvia*, **200**
Chopin, 20
Choreography, 87-90, 121-3, 160
Cimarosa, 25
Clair, Stella, in *The Rake's Progress*, **80;** in *The Haunted Ballroom*, **81**
Clark, Sir Kenneth, 133
Clavé, 138
Clayden, Pauline, in *Bonne Bouche*, **102;** in *Daphnis and Chloé*, **194**
Clegg, Peter, in *Sylvia*, **113**
Cocteau, Jean, 25, 27, 30, 138
Coliseum Theatre, London, 18-22, 28
Costumes and Sets, **139 to 157**
Covent Garden, Royal Opera House, 14, 16, 18, 25-8, **29,** 32-4, 73; Royal Command Performance at, 73, 74; Sadler's Wells Ballet at, 87, **91-116,** 118-20; décor at, 135-8; New Theatre Royal in 1810, **120**
Cranko, John, 89, 136, **177**
Craxton, John, 138
Cruickshank, George, 29
Cruickshank, Robert, 29, 32

d'Albaicin, Maria, in *Schéhérazade*, 27, in *Cuadro Flamenco*, 28
Dalcroze Eurhythmics, **69**
Dale, Margaret, in *Wedding Bouquet*, **114**
Dandré, M. Victor, 65
Danilova, 28, 32; in *Boutique Fantasque*, 88
d'Annunzio, Gabriel, 18
Dargomijsky, 31
Dauberval, 58
de Basil, Colonel, 33, 87, 88
de Falla, 24

de Glehn, 18
de Valois, Ninette, 28, 33, 34, 43, 74, 87, 88, 117, **131,** 136, 158-60, **161, 162, 166, 179;** founder of Sadler's Wells, 56-63; in *The Jackdaw and the Pigeons*, **37;** in *Pride*, **37;** in *Douanes*, **39, 41;** in *Coppelia*, **42;** in *Barabau*, **45;** in *The Wedding Bouquet*, .53 .
Debussy, 15
Décor and Costumes, 18-27, 45, 90, 133-8, **139 to 157**
Delaunay, Robert, 19
Delaunay, Sonia, 19
Delibes, 31, 119, 137
Delius' *Paris*, 118
Derain, André, 22, 23, 24, 134, 135
Diaghilev, Serge, 14, 17-21, **21,** 22-30, **30,** 31-4, 53, 55, 57, 60, 74, 88, 159, 160; music for, 117, 118; décors for, 133-5, 138
Dolin, Anton, **26,** 33, 58; in *La Belle au Bois Dormant*, 26; in *Douanes*, **41**
Donizetti, 118
Drage, Mary, 90
Drama, Classical, 158
Drury Lane Theatre, London, 15, 16
Dublin, Abbey Theatre, 57
Dubrovska, 28
Dupré, Louis, 58

Edinburgh Festival, 32
Elssler, 58
Elvin, Violetta, 90, **162;** in *Daphnis and Chloé*, **108;** in *Swan Lake*, **183**
Empire Theatre, London, 23, 25, 27, 33
Evans, Edwin, **127**

Farron, Julia, in *Daphnis and Chloé*, **197**
Fedorovitch, Sophie, 135, 137, **152**
Field, John, in *Swan Lake*, **183, 190**
Fifield, Elaine, 90; in *Blood Wedding*, **79;** in *Pineapple Poll*, **82;** in *Coppelia*, **83;** in *Reflection*, **196**
Flaxman, 152
Florence (Italy), 13, 29
Fokine, Michael, **57,** 58, 89
Fonteyn, Margot, 34, **35,** 90, **167, 179;** in *The Haunted Ballroom*, 43; in *Barabau*, **45;** in *Pomona*, **48;** in *Les Patineurs*, **49;** in *Façade*, **52;** in *The Sleeping Princess*, **54;** in *The Sleeping Beauty*, 74, **170, 172;** in *The Firebird*, **91, 95;** in *Tiresias*, **101, 170;** in *Daphnis and Chloé*, **109;** in *Sylvia*, **112, 171;** in *Dante Sonata*, **115;** in *Les Sirènes*, **168;** in *Apparitions*, **169;** in *Ballet Imperial*, **179**
Franck's *Symphonic Variations*, 118
French Court, 158
Fry, Roger, 16

Gardel, 58
Garrick, David, 158

Gautier, Théophile, 55
Gielgud, Sir John, 158
Gilbert, Jean, **130**
Gill, David, in *Blood Wedding*, **79**
Gissy, 133
Glazounov, 19
Glinka, 31
Goncharova, 15
Goossens, Eugene, 26
Gordon, Gavin, 118
Gore, Walter, in *Coppelia*, **42**; in *The Rake's Progress*, **44**; in *Barabau*, **45**
Gounod, 28, 31
Goya, 24
Gozzoli, Benozzo, 24
Grant, Alexander, in *Don Quixote*, **97**; in *Ballabile*, **97, 192**; in *Donald of the Burthens*, **103**; in *Sylvia*, **113**
Greenwood, John, in *Coppelia*, **42**
Grey, Beryl, 90, **185**; in *Donald of the Burthens*, **103**; in *Cinderlla*, **110**; in *Ballet Imperial*, **179**
Gris, Juan, 134
Grock, 19
Guimard, 58

Hart, John, **191**; in *Sylvia*, **113**
Haskell, Arnold L. (The Sadler's Wells School), 55-72, **67, 71**
Heaton, Anne, in *Giselle*, **199**
Helpmann, Robert, 34, 89, 135; in *The Jar*, **41**; in *Apparitions*, **53**; in *The Sleeping Princess*, **54**; in *The Prospect Before Us*, 87, **173**; in *Wedding Bouquet*, **114, 174**; in *Hamlet*, 137; in *Sleeping Beauty*, **170, 174**; in *Miracle in the Gorbals*, **174**; in *Comus*, **174**; in *Job*, **175**
Hightower, Rosella, 90
Hill, Stuart, 18
Hindemith, 33
Hogan, Michael, in *Sea Change*, **77**
Hogarth's *The Rake's Progress*, **139**
Holden, Stanley, in *Harlequin in April*, **78**
Hollingsworth, John, **130**
Horner, Mary, in *Les Patineurs*, **49**
Howard, Andrée, 89, **178**
Hurok, Sol, **179**
Hurry, Leslie, 137, 150, 151

Idzikowski, 46; in *The Good Humoured Ladies*, 18; in *Carnaval*, 20; in *La Belle au Bois Dormant*, 20; in *Children's Tales*, 20; in *Les Rendezvous*, 40
Ironside, Robin, 137
Ironside, Robin and Christopher, 154
Irving, Robert, 117, **131**
Islington, Sadler's Wells Ballet at, 73; development of ballet at, 87
Ivanov, 87

Jackson, Rowena, 90; in *Swan Lake*, **186**
Johannsen, 55, 58
Jones, Inigo, 133
Judson, Stanley, in *Coppelia*, **42**

Kandinsky, 136
Karsavina, Tamara, 16, 55, 56; in *Le Spectre de la Rose*, 14; in *l'Oiseau de Feu*, 14, 15; in *Carnaval*, **18**
Kaufer, MacKnight, 136
Kchessinska, 55
Kean, Edmund, 16
Keane, Fiorella, in *Bonne Bouche*, **102**
King Alfonso of Spain, 17
King Edward VII, 14
Kochno, Boris, 28, 29
Koribut-Kubitovitch, Pavel, 31

Lamb, Henry, 20
Lambert, Constant, 31, 33, 34, 53, 117, 118, **125, 126, 127**; at Sadler's Wells School, 58
Lancaster, Osbert, 138, 155, 156, 157
Lane, Maryon, in *Sea Change*, **77**; in *Coppelia*, **84**
Larionov, 20
Larsen, Gerd, in *Façade*, **51**
Lebrun, President and Madame, 73, 74
Legat, 58
Legrand, Louis, 62
Lepape, 16
Lepeschinskaia, 90
Lepri, Giovanni, 58
Lesley, June, in *Bonne Bouche*, **102**
Levitsky, 32
Lewis, Wyndham, 28, 31
Lichine, in *Présages*, 88
Lifar, Serge, 21, 28, 29
Lindsay, Rosemary, in *The Shadow*, **198**
Liszt, 118
Lopokova, Lydia, 25; in *The Good Humoured Ladies*, 18-20; in *Carnaval*, 20; in *La Belle au Bois Dormant*, 20, 26; in *Coppelia*, **42**; in *Façade*, 50
Lully, 55
Lyceum Theatre, London, 29

Macarthy, Sheila, in *The Rake's Progress*, **44**
McCutcheon, Miss L., 60, **71**
Madrid, 17
Malone, Mrs. L'Estrange, 60
Markova, Alicia, 32, 33, 57, 58, 74; in *Giselle* **33, 163**; in *Les Rendezvous*, **40**; in *The Haunted Ballroom*, **43**; in *The Rake's Progress*, **44**
Massine, Leonide, 25, 31, 33, 88, **166, 176**; in *Cléopatre*, 19; in *The Good Humoured Ladies*, 18-20; in *The Midnight Sun*, 20; in *La Boutique Fantasque*, 23; in *Le Tricorne*, 24, 88; in *Beau Danube*, 88

Matisse, Henri, 25, 134
May, Pamela, in *The Gods Go A-Begging*, **48**; in *Façade*, **51**; in *Bonne Bouche*, **102**; in *Dante Sonata*, **115, 182**
Méhul, 31
Melliss, Peggy, in *Façade*, **51**
Mercury Theatre, 33
Messel, Oliver, 26, 74, 137, 153
Metliss, Maurice, in *Blood Wedding*, **79**
Meyerbeer, 118
Milhaud, 43, 118
Miller, Elizabeth, in *The Gods Go A-Begging*, **38**; in *Les Patineurs*, **49**
Miller, Patricia, **85**; in *Harlequin in April*, **78**
Molière, 55
Monahan, James, 73
Mordkin, 14
Moreton, Ursula, **86**; at Sadler's Wells School, 60, **71**; in *Casse-Noisette*, **38**; in *The Haunted Ballroom*, **43**; in *Création du Monde*, **43**
Moscow, 56
Moussorgsky, 15, 31
Mozart, 118
Music and the Ballet, 33, 117-24, **125-31**, 160

Negus, Anne, in *Ballabile*, **97**
Nemchinova, in *La Belle au Bois Dormant*, 26
Neo-classicism, 88, 89, 90
Nerina, Nadia, 90, **184**; in *Don Quixote*, **97**
Newton, Joy, in *Job*, 38; in *The Rake's Progress*, **44**; in *The Gods Go A-Begging*, **48**
Nijinska, in *La Belle au Bois Dormant*, 26; in *Panorama*, 28
Nijinski, 16, 35, 55, 133, 134; in *Le Spectre de la Rose*, 14; in *l'Oiseau de Feu*, 14; in *Carnaval*, 20
Nikitina, 28
Noverre, Jean-Georges, 58, 158

Opera, 119, 123; contemporary, 158
Opera Houses: acoustics in, Chicago, Covent Garden, Milan, Vienna, 120
Operas: *La Bohème*, 15; *Electra*, 120; *Khovantchina*, 15; *Nozze di Figaro*, 16; *The Ring*, 120; *William Tell*, 23; *Wozzeck*, 120
O'Reilly, Sheila, in *Khadra*, **76**

Page, Annette, in *The Haunted Ballroom*, **81**
Palace Theatre, London, 14
Paris, 134; Chatelet Théâtre, 14; Académie Royale, 58
Pavlova, Anna, 14, 35, 55, 58, 65; in *Les Sylphides*, **56**
Pécourt, Louis, 58
Pergolesi, 25
Perrault, 137
Petipa, 55, 57, 87, 88, 137, 159
Petit, Roland, **176**

Phillips, Ailne, at Sadler's Wells School, 60, **71**; in *Les Rendezvous*, **40**
Picasso, 15, 24, 25, 134, 135, 137, 138
Piper, John, 135, 136, 146
Planté, François, 23
Pollock, Mr. Benjamin, 28
Poole, David, in *Sea Change*, **77**; in *Blood Wedding*, **79**; in *The Haunted Ballroom*, **81**; in *Pineapple Poll*, **82**; in *Coppelia*, **83**
Poulenc, 25, 28
Prince Antioch Cantemir, 32
Princes Theatre, London, 25, 74
Princess Margaret, 35; visits Sadler's Wells School, 64, **67**
Prokofiev, 25
Purcell, 118
Pushkin, 32

Queen Alexandra, 14

Rambert, Marie, 33, 58
Rameau, 55
Rassine, Alexis, in *The Blue Bird*, **189**
Raynouard, 66
Respighi, 23
Riabouchinska, in *Choreartium*, 88
Richmond Park, The White Lodge, **64**
Rimsky-Korsakov, 19
Roberts, William, 28
Rodrigues, Alfred, **178**
Roseingrave, Thomas, 31
Rossini, 23, 24, 31
Rouault, 134
Rowlandson, 31
Royal Command Performance at Covent Garden, 73, 74
Royal Opera House, Covent Garden (see Covent Garden)
Rubinstein, Anton, 30
Rumbold, Hugo, 16
Russian Ballet, 14, 15, 16, 20, 27, 28, 55, 56, 59, 117, 134, 135; effect of Russian Revolution on, 18

Sadler's Wells Ballet, 33, 34, 73, 74, 87-90, **91-116**; 135, 138, 158; beginning, 33; early days, **37-54**
Sadler's Wells Opera Company, 33
Sadler's Wells School, 13, 35, 55-72; general education at, 35, 59-65
Sadler's Wells Theatre, 117, 118, 137; in 1792, **119**
Sadler's Wells Theatre Ballet, **75-86**, 138
Sallé, 58
Satie, Erik, 25, 31
Scarlatti, Domenico, 19, 31
Schubert, 28; *Wanderer Fantasy*, **118**
Schumann, 15

Seraphine, 58
Sergeeff, 57
Serov, Valentin, 56, 57
Sert, José-Maria, 15, 25
Sets and Costumes, **139** to **157**
Shabelevsky, in *Les Matelots*, 88; in *Cotillon*, 88
Shadwick, Joseph, 117
Shaw, Brian, in *Sylvia*, **113**; in *Les Patineurs*, **193**
Shearer, Moira, 34, 90; in *La Boutique Fantasque*, 23; in *Façade*, **52**; in *Cinderella*, **110, 111, 181**; in *Wedding Bouquet*, **114**; in *Swan Lake*, **180**
Shervashidze, Prince, 31
Sitwell, Sacheverell, 13
Sokolova, Lydia, 32; in *Children's Tales*, 20; in *La Belle au Bois Dormant*, 26
Somes, Michael, **187**; in *The Firebird*, **93, 96**; in *Daphnis and Chloé*, **108, 109**; in *Cinderella*, **111**; in *Sylvia*, **112, 113, 188**; in *Dante Sonata*, **115**; in *Swan Lake*, **186**
Spanish dancing, 24, and costumes, 25
Sparger, Miss, 62
Spessiva, in *La Belle au Bois Dormant*, 26
Spessivtseva, 55
Stein, Gertrude, 53, **127**
Strachey, Lytton, 20, 28
Stravinsky, Igor, 15, 22, 25, 27, 28, 118, 138
Stravinsky, Soulima, 23
Sutherland, Graham, 135, 147
St. Petersburg, 22, 26, 32, 56

Taglioni, 58
Tallchief, Maria, 90
Taylor, Valerie, 64
Tchaikowsky, 14, 27, 28, 30, 33, 118, 119
Tchernicheva, Lubor, in *Cléopatre*, 19
Thellusson, Doris, 60
Tiepolo, Domenico, 25
Toklas, Alice, B., 53

Toumanova, 32
Toye, 118
Trecu, Pirmin, **85**; in *Blood Wedding*, **79**; in *Coppelia*, **84**
Trefilova, 55
Tudor, in *Douanes*, **41**
Turner, Harold, in *Barabau*, **45**; in *The Gods Go A-Begging*, **48**; in *Les Patineurs*, **49**; at Sadler's Wells School, **68**

Ulanova, 90
Utrillo, 134

Vaganova, 58
Van Praag, Peggy, **86**
Venice, Diaghilev in, 18, 29, 30, 32
Verchinina, in *Présages*, 88
Vernon, Gilbert, in *Bonne Bouche*, **102**
Veronese, Paul, 15
Vigano, 58
Vlakevitch, 138
Voltaire, 55

Wadsworth, Edward, 28
Wagner, 27
Walton, Sir William, 31, 118, **129**
Warsaw, 56
Webb, H. J., 29
Webster, David, **89**
Whistler, Rex, 32, 73, 132, 136, 139-42, **142**
Wilde, Oscar, 30
Williams, Vaughan, 118, **128**
Woffington, Peg, 16
Wollheim, Mr., 31
Wolmark, Alfred, 19
Wood, Christopher, 30
Woodhouse, Mrs. Gordon, 19, 31

Zucchi, 58